Simply Shakespeare

Original Shakespearean Text
With a Modern Line-for-Line Translation

ROMEO & JULIET

All inquiries should be addressed to:
Barron's Educational Series, Inc.
250 Wireless Boulevard
Hauppauge, New York 11788
http://www.barronseduc.com

ISBN-13: 978-0-7641-2085-5
ISBN-10: 0-7641-2085-9

Library of Congress Catalog Card No. 2001043310

Library of Congress Cataloging-in-Publication Data

Shakespeare, William, 1564–1616.
    Romeo and Juliet / edited and rendered into modern English by Jenny Mueller.
        p. cm. — (Simply Shakespeare)
    Includes bibliographical references.
    Summary: Presents the original text of Shakespeare's play side by side with a modern version, with discussion questions, role-playing scenarios, and other study activities.
    ISBN 0-7641-2085-9
        1. Verona (Italy)Juvenile drama. 2. Vendetta—Juvenile drama. 3. Youth—Juvenile drama. 4. Children's plays, English. [1. Shakespeare, William, 1564–1616. Romeo and Juliet. 2. Plays. 3. English literature—History and criticism.] I. Mueller, Jenny, 1962– II. Title.
    PR2831 .A25 2002
    822.3'3—dc21
                                                                2001043310

PRINTED IN CHINA
18

Simply Shakespeare

Titles in the Series

Contents

Introduction

William Shakespeare, 1564–1616

Who was William Shakespeare? This simple question has challenged scholars for years. The man behind vivid, unforgettable characters like Hamlet, Romeo and Juliet, and King Lear is a shadow compared to his creations. Luckily, official records of Shakespeare's time have preserved some facts about his life.

Shakespeare was born in April 1564 in Stratford-upon-Avon, England. His father, John Shakespeare, was a prominent local merchant. Shakespeare probably attended grammar school in Stratford, learning basic Latin and Greek and studying works by ancient Roman writers. In 1582, when Shakespeare was 18, he married Anne Hathaway. Eventually, the couple had three children—but, like many families in their day, they were forced to endure a tragic loss when Hamnet, their only son, died at age 11.

No records document Shakespeare's life from 1585 to 1592, when he was between the ages of 21 and 28. In his writings, Shakespeare seems to know so much about so many things that it's tempting to make guesses about how he supported his young family during this period. Over the years, it's been speculated that he worked as a schoolteacher, a butcher, or an actor—and even that he did a little poaching as a young man. Thanks to some London theater gossip left behind by a professional rival, we know that Shakespeare was living in London as a playwright and actor by 1592. Meanwhile, Anne and the children stayed in Stratford.

This must have been a thrilling time for Shakespeare. In 1592, England was becoming a powerful nation under its great and clever queen, Elizabeth I. English explorers and colonists crossed seas to search strange new worlds. London was a bustling, exciting center of commerce, full of travelers from abroad. And though many Europeans still looked down on English culture, they admitted that London's stages boasted some of the best plays and actors to be found. Travelers from all over admired the dramas of Christopher Marlowe, Thomas Kyd, and the new name on the scene, William Shakespeare.

Nevertheless, the life of the theater had its hazards. London's actors, playwrights, and theatrical entrepreneurs chose a risky and somewhat shady line of work. Religious leaders condemned the theater for encouraging immorality and idleness among the London populace. London's city leaders, fearful of crowds, closed the theaters in times of unrest or plague. Luckily, the London troupes had some powerful "fans"—members of the nobility who acted as patrons, protecting the troupes from their enemies. Queen Elizabeth herself loved plays. Special performances were regularly given for her at court.

By 1594, two theatrical companies had emerged as the most popular. Archrivals, The Lord Admiral's Men and The Lord Chamberlain's Men performed at the Rose and the Theatre, respectively. However, The Lord Chamberlain's Men had an ace: Shakespeare was both a founding member and the company's main playwright. The company's fine lead actor was Richard Burbage, the first man to play such roles as Hamlet, Othello, and Macbeth. With a one-two punch like that, it's not surprising that The Lord Chamberlain's Men soon emerged as London's top troupe. By 1597, Shakespeare had written such works as *Romeo and Juliet, The Merchant of Venice,* and *A Midsummer Night's Dream.* His finances grew with his reputation, and he was able to buy land and Stratford's second-largest house, where Anne and the children moved while he remained in London.

Then as now, owning property went a long way. Like many acting companies to this day, The Lord Chamberlain's Men got involved in a bitter dispute with their landlord. However, they owned the actual timbers of the Theatre building—which turned out to be useful assets. Eventually the exasperated troupe hired a builder to secretly take apart the Theatre, then transported its timbers across London to the south bank of the River Thames. There, they used the Theatre's remains to construct their new home—The Globe.

At The Globe, many of Shakespeare's greatest plays first came to life. From 1599 until his death in 1616, the open-air Globe served as Shakespeare's main stage. Audiences saw the first performances of *Hamlet, Macbeth, Twelfth Night,* and *King Lear* there. (In winter, Shakespeare's company performed at London's Blackfriars, the indoor theater that housed the first performance of *The Tempest.*) In 1603, after the death of Queen Elizabeth, Shakespeare's troupe added a new triumph to its résumé. Changing its name to The King's Men, it became the official theatrical company of England's new monarch, James I. The company performed frequently at court and state functions for its powerful new patron.

Around 1611–1612, Shakespeare returned permanently to Stratford. Unfortunately, we know little about his domestic life there. Where Shakespeare is concerned, there's no "tell-all" biography to reveal his intimate life. Was he happily wed to Anne, or did he live for so long in London to escape a bad marriage? Do the sonnets Shakespeare published in 1609 tell us a real-life story of his relationships with a young man, a "Dark Lady," and a rival for the lady's love? What were Shakespeare's political beliefs? From his writings, it's clear that Shakespeare understood life's best and worst emotions very deeply. But we'll never know how much of his own life made its way into his art. He died at the age of 53 on April 23, 1616, leaving behind the almost 40 plays and scores of poems that have spoken for him to generations of readers and listeners. Shakespeare is buried in Holy Trinity Church in Stratford, where he lies under a stone that warns the living—in verse—never to disturb his bones.

Shakespeare's Theater

Going to a play in Shakespeare's time was a completely different experience than going to a play today. How theaters were built, who attended, what happened during the performance, and who produced the plays were all quite unlike most theater performances today.

Theaters in Shakespeare's time were mainly outside the walls of the city of London—and away from the authorities *in* London. In those times, many religious authorities (especially radical Protestants) condemned plays and playgoing. They preached that plays, being stage illusions, were acts of deception and therefore sinful. The city authorities in London agreed that the theaters encouraged immorality. Despite this, theaters did exist in and around the city of London. They were, however, housed in neighborhoods known as Liberties. Liberties were areas that previously had religious functions and therefore were under the control of the crown, not the city of London. Luckily for playgoers, the monarchs Elizabeth and James were more tolerant of the amusements offered by the stage than the London authorities.

Who enjoyed what the stage had to offer? Almost all of London society went to the theater. Merchants and their wives, prostitutes, lawyers, laborers, and visitors from other countries would attend. Once you were at the theater, your social station dictated what you could pay and where you sat. If you could only afford a pence (about a penny), you would stand in the yard immediately surrounding the stage.

(These members of Shakespeare's audience were called "groundlings.")
As many as a thousand other spectators might join you there. In the
yard everyone would be exposed to the weather and to peddlers selling
fruit and nuts. Your experience would probably be more active and less
quiet than attending a play today. Movement was not uncommon. If
you wanted a better or different view, you might rove about the yard. If
you paid another pence, you could move into a lower gallery.

The galleries above and surrounding the stage on all sides could
accommodate up to 2,000 more people. However, because the galleries
were vertical and surrounded the stage, no matter where you sat, you
would never be more than 35 feet away from the stage. The galleries
immediately behind the stage were reserved for members of the nobility and royalty. From behind the stage a noble could not only see
everything, but—more importantly—could be seen by others in the
audience! Queen Elizabeth and King James were less likely to attend a
theater performance, although they protected theater companies.
Instead, companies performed plays for them at court.

The Globe's stage was similar to the other outdoor theaters in
Shakespeare's time. These stages offered little decoration or frills.
Consequently, the actors and the text carried the burden of delivering
the drama. Without the help of scenery or lighting, the audience had
to imagine what was not represented on the stage (the storms, ship-
wrecks, and so forth). The Globe's stage was rectangular—with dimen-
sions of about 27 by 44 feet. At the back of the stage was a curtained
wall containing three entrances onto the stage. These entrances led
directly from the tiring (as in "attiring") house, where the actors would
dress. The middle entrance was covered by a hanging tapestry and was
probably used for special entrances—such as a ceremonial procession
or the delivery of a prologue.

Unlike the yard, the stage was covered by a canopied roof that was
suspended by two columns. This canopy was known as the *heavens*. Its
underside was covered with paintings of the sun, moon, stars, and sky
and was visible to all theatergoers. *Hell* was the area below the stage
with a trapdoor as the entrance. Immediately behind and one flight
above the stage were the dressing rooms, and above them lay the stor-
age area for props and costumes.

Indoor theaters were similar to outdoor theaters in many respects.
They featured a bare stage with the heavens, a trapdoor leading to hell,
and doors leading to the tiring house. Builders created indoor theaters
from preexisting space in already constructed buildings. These theaters
were smaller, and because they were in town they were also more

expensive. Standing in the yard of an outdoor theater cost a pence. The cheapest seat in an *indoor* theater was sixpence. The most fashionable and wealthy members of London society attended indoor theaters as much to see as to be seen. If you were a gallant (a fashionable theater-goer), you could pay 24 pence and actually sit on a stool at the edge of the stage—where everyone could see you.

The actors' costumes were also on display. Whether plays were performed indoors or outdoors, costumes were richly decorated. They were one of the main assets of a theater company and one of the draws of theater. However, costumes didn't necessarily match the period of the play's setting. How spectacular the costumes looked was more important than how realistic they were or if they matched the period setting.

These costumes were worn on stage only by men or boys who were a part of licensed theater companies. The actors in the companies were exclusively male and frequently doubled up on parts. Boys played female roles before their voices changed. Some actors were also share-holders—the most important members of a theater company. The shareholders owned the company's assets (the play texts, costumes, and props) and made a profit from the admissions gathered. Besides the shareholders and those actors who did not hold shares, other company members were apprentices and hired men and musicians.

The actors in Shakespeare's day worked hard. They were paid according to the house's take. New plays were staged rapidly, possibly with as little as three weeks from the time a company first received the play text until opening night. All the while, the companies appeared to have juggled a large number of new and older plays in performance. In lead roles, the most popular actors might have delivered as many as 4,000 lines in six different plays during a London working week! Working at this pace, it seems likely that teamwork was key to a company's success.

The Sound of Shakespeare

Shakespeare's heroes and heroines all share one quality: They're all great talkers. They combine Shakespeare's powerful imagery and vocabulary with a sound that thunders, trills, rocks, and sings.

When Shakespearean actors say their lines, they don't just speak lines of dialogue. Often, they're also speaking lines of dramatic poetry that are written in a sound pattern called *iambic pentameter*. When these lines don't rhyme and are not grouped in stanzas, they're called *blank verse*. Though many passages in Shakespeare plays are written in prose, the most important and serious moments are almost always in iambic pentameter. As Shakespeare matured, the sound of his lines began to change. Late plays like *The Tempest* are primarily in a wonderfully flowing blank verse. Earlier works, such as *Romeo and Juliet,* feature much more rhymed iambic pentameter, often with punctuation at the end of each line to make the rhymes even stronger.

Terms like "iambic pentameter" sound scarily technical—like part of a chemistry experiment that will blow up the building if you measure it wrong. But the Greeks, who invented iambic pentameter, used it as a dance beat. Later writers no longer used it as something one could literally shimmy to, but it was still a way to organize the rhythmic noise and swing of speech. An *iamb* contains one unaccented (or unstressed) syllable and one accented (stressed) syllable, in that order. It borrows from the natural swing of our heartbeats to go *ker-THUMP, ker-THUMP*. Five of these ker-thumping units in a row make a line of iambic *penta*meter.

Dance or rock music needs a good, regular thumping of drums (or drum machine) and bass to get our feet tapping and bodies dancing, but things can get awfully monotonous if that's all there is to the sound. Poetry works the same way. With its ten syllables and five ker-thumps, a line like "he WENT to TOWN toDAY to BUY a CAR" is perfect iambic pentameter. It's just as regular as a metronome. But it isn't poetry. "In SOOTH/ I KNOW/ not WHY/ I AM/ so SAD" is poetry (*The Merchant of Venice,* Act 1, Scene 1). Writers like Shakespeare change the iambic pentameter pattern of their blank verse all the time to keep things sounding interesting. The melody of vowels and other sound effects makes the lines even more musical and varied. As it reaches the audience's ears, this mix of basic, patterned beat and sound variations carries powerful messages of meaning and emotion. The beating, regular rhythms of blank verse also help actors remember their lines.

Why did Shakespeare use this form? Blank verse dominated through a combination of novelty, tradition, and ease. The Greeks and Romans passed on a tradition of combining poetry and drama. English playwrights experimented with this tradition by using all sorts of verse and prose for their plays. By the 1590s, blank verse had caught on with some of the best new writers in London. In the hands of writers like the popular Christopher Marlowe and the up-and-coming Will Shakespeare, it was more than just the latest craze in on-stage sound.

Blank verse also fit well with the English language itself. Compared to languages like French and Italian, English is hard to rhyme. It's also heavily accentual—another way of saying that English really bumps and thumps.

The words and sounds coming from the stage were new and thrilling to Shakespeare's audience. England was falling in love with its own language. English speakers were still making up grammar, spelling, and pronunciation as they went along—giving the language more of a "hands-on" feel than it has today. The grammar books and dictionaries that finally fixed the "rules" of English did not appear until after Shakespeare's death. The language grew and grew, soaking up words from other languages, combining and making new words. Politically, the country also grew in power and pride.

Shakespeare's language reflects this sense of freedom, experimentation, and power. When he put his words in the beat of blank verse and the mouths of London's best actors, it must have sounded a little like the birth of rock and roll—mixing old styles and new sounds to make a new, triumphant swagger.

Publishing Shakespeare

Books of Shakespeare's plays come in all shapes and sizes. They range from slim paperbacks like this one to heavy, muscle-building anthologies of his collected works. Libraries devote shelves of space to works by and about "the Bard." Despite all that paper and ink, no printed text of a Shakespeare play can claim to be an exact, word-by-word copy of what Shakespeare wrote.

Today, most writers work on computers and can save their work electronically. Students everywhere know the horror of losing the only copy of something they've written and make sure they always have a backup version! In Shakespeare's time, a playwright delivered a handwritten copy of his work to the acting company that asked him to write a play. This may have been his only copy—which was now the property of the company, not the writer. In general, plays were viewed as mere "entertainments"—not literary art. They were written quickly and were often disposed of when the acting companies had no more use for them.

The draft Shakespeare delivered was a work in progress. He and the company probably added, deleted, and changed some material—stage directions, entrances and exits, even lines and character names—during rehearsals. Companies may have had a clean copy written out by a scribe (a professional hand-writer) or by the writer himself. Most likely they kept this house copy for future performances. No copies of Shakespeare's plays in his own handwriting have survived.

Acting companies might perform a hit play for years before it was printed, usually in small books called *quartos.* However, the first published versions of Shakespeare's plays vary considerably. Some of these texts are thought to be of an inferior, incomplete quality. Because of this, scholars have speculated that they are not based on authoritative, written copies, but were re-created from actors' memories or from the shorthand notes of a scribe working for a publisher.

Shakespearean scholars often call these apparently faulty versions of his plays "bad quartos." Why might such texts have appeared? Scholars have guessed that they are "pirated versions." They believe that acting companies tried to keep their plays out of print to prevent rival troupes from stealing popular material. However, booksellers sometimes printed unauthorized versions of Shakespeare's plays that were used by competing companies. The pirated versions may have been done with help from actors who had played minor roles in the play, memorized it, and then sold their unreliable, memorized versions. (In recent years, this theory has been challenged by some scholars who argue that the "bad" quartos may be based on Shakespeare's own first drafts or that they reliably reflect early performance texts of the plays.)

"Good" quartos were printed with the permission of the company that owned the play and were based on written copies. However, even these authorized versions were far from perfect. The printers had to work either by deciphering the playwright's handwriting or by using a flawed version printed earlier. They also had to memorize lines as they manually set type on the press. And they decided how a line should be punctuated and spelled—not always with foolproof judgment!

The first full collection of Shakespeare's plays came out in 1623, seven years after his death. Called the "First Folio," this collection included 36 plays compiled by John Heminge and Henry Condell, actor-friends of Shakespeare from The King's Men troupe.

To develop the First Folio texts, Heminge, Condell, and their co-editors probably worked with a mix of handwritten and both good and bad printed versions of their friend's plays. Their 1623 version had many errors, and though later editions of that text corrected some mistakes, they also added new ones. The First Folio also contained no indications of where acts and scenes began and ended. The scene and act divisions that appear standard in most modern editions of Shakespeare actually rely on the shrewd guesses of generations of editors and researchers.

Most modern editors of Shakespeare depend on a combination of trustworthy early publications to come up with the most accurate text possible. They often use the versions in the First Folio, its later editions, and other "good," authorized publications of single plays. In some cases, they also consult "bad" versions or rely on pure guesswork to decide the most likely reading of some words or lines. Because of such uncertainties, modern editions of Shakespeare often vary, depending on editors' research and choices. This version of William Shakespeare's *Romeo and Juliet* is taken from the Quarto of 1599.

Romeo and Juliet

Introduction to the Play

Who are the world's greatest lovers? Antony and Cleopatra. Dante and Beatrice. Superman and Lois Lane. Romeo and Juliet.

Thanks to William Shakespeare, the names "Romeo and Juliet" are practically synonyms for passionate, mutual love. Although Shakespeare did not invent this story of youthful passion (see the "Sources" section), it's Shakespeare's *Romeo and Juliet* that turned the title lovers into classic models for tragic romance.

In a way, this fact is dangerous for Shakespeare's play. Audiences might come to *Romeo and Juliet* expecting a nice, sentimental soap opera. Instead, they find a world full of complex emotions, gorgeous poetry, and wonderful observation—*plus* lots of high romance and dramatic excitement.

Written around 1595, *Romeo and Juliet* marks a new stage for Shakespeare. Up until then, Shakespeare had written mainly comedies and plays that dealt with English history. He was also well known for his narrative poems. *Romeo and Juliet* was one of his first tragedies.

As a tragedy, *Romeo and Juliet* is adventurous. The teenage main characters come from socially prominent families. However, they are not members of the nobility. Shakespeare was quite daring in making such relatively normal people the focus of a tragic play. It was also unusual for tragedies to center on a love story. Lovers usually got together in comedies, while tragedies focused on the struggles and failures of individuals. (Many of the great tragedies Shakespeare wrote afterwards *do* focus on a single main character, as in *Hamlet* or *King Lear*.)

Romeo and Juliet also gave Shakespeare an early chance to show off his flair for mixing comedy, tragedy, and romance in one play. This talent reached its heights in some of his last, magical plays—works like *The Tempest*. In *Romeo and Juliet,* Shakespeare also began to alter his poetic style and use of imagery. As the play progresses, its lines change from a formal, rhyming style to a more natural and flexible blank verse. Like Romeo himself, Shakespeare begins to use words in a way that's not so "by the book."

Romeo and Juliet sets young against old, love against hate, and wisdom against passion. Shakespeare's imagery helps convey this sense of extremes by weaving a pattern of natural opposites, such as light and dark, high and low, night and day. Like lovers and like deadly enemies, these opposites both clash and complement each other.

In the beginning of this play, this imagery deliberately imitates some of the conventional love poetry of Shakespeare's time. As the play goes on, it begins to mesh more and more with the play's themes and plot, drawing us further into Romeo and Juliet's world of love and conflict. Images of fire, blood, and lightning add to the sense of vivid intensity. Audiences really *feel* those hot days and cool dawns in the Italian summer. Shakespeare's images help to deepen and develop the emotion in this story of star-crossed love. Fate, coincidence, and mischance all play roles in the unfolding drama.

Scholars think Romeo and Juliet was first performed by The Lord Chamberlain's Men at the venue called simply the Theatre. Then as now, it appears to have been one of Shakespeare's most popular plays.

Romeo and Juliet's Sources

In the 1999 hit movie Shakespeare in Love, the young playwright is seen composing a play called Romeo and Ethel, the Pirate's Daughter. With a little help from a new love interest and a rival playwright, Shakespeare slowly transforms his pirate adventure into Romeo and Juliet.

It's a fun story. But to get closer to the truth of how Romeo and Juliet was written, the moviemakers would have had to show Shakespeare poring over his books. In particular, they would have had to have portrayed him reading a long and fairly boring poem called The Tragical History of Romeus and Juliet, published in 1562 by Arthur Broke (sometimes spelled Brooke).

Shakespeare took most of his plot from Broke. He made some important changes, however, including narrowing the action to just a few short days, making Mercutio a major character, and making the Nurse more comically likeable. Most important, he got rid of Broke's moralizing tone, which sternly disapproves of the pair's lovemaking and impulsiveness. Shakespeare's poetry changed Broke's sermon into a glorious rhapsody.

Broke didn't make up the story either. He got it from Pierre Boaistuau's French translation (in Histoire Tragiques, 1559) of an Italian story by Matteo Bandello that was published in 1554. Bandello, in turn, borrowed parts of his plot from still earlier Italian versions—one of which actually *did* contain some pirates!

Every year, thousands of visitors to Verona, Italy, flock to local attractions like "Juliet's House," "Juliet's Balcony," and "Juliet's Tomb." Despite this fact, there's precious little evidence that *Romeo and Juliet* tells a true story. Luckily for Verona's tourist bureau, Shakespeare's wonderful version of this old Italian tale means that, whether they were real or not, Romeo and Juliet will never be forgotten.

The Text of *Romeo and Juliet*

The first version of Shakespeare's play was published in 1597, but this version may be quite untrustworthy. Many Shakespeare scholars think the 1597 version is a "bad quarto"—the work of a shady publisher and some actors who had appeared in the road version of the popular play, then used their memories to "pirate" the text to make some fast cash. (Some scholars disagree with this theory and think that the text shows an early version of the play as it was once performed.)

Two years later, a new version appeared that claimed to be "newly corrected, augmented, and amended." It was also nearly twice as long. Possibly hurried into print by Shakespeare's company to counteract the 1597 text, this 1599 edition is the one that editors now rely upon as the most authoritative version. It was probably printed from Shakespeare's own handwritten manuscript. However, the printer appears to have relied on the 1597 "bad" version when Shakespeare's writing was illegible. Editors today also look to the bad version for help with stage directions, which are more detailed in the pirated text.

All the early versions of the play contain some printers' errors and inconsistencies, as well as other textual problems. Modern editions of *Romeo and Juliet* solve these problems in different ways, based on their editors' research and educated guesses. As with all of Shakespeare's plays, today's editions of *Romeo and Juliet* vary depending on such editorial choices.

Romeo and Juliet

Original text and modern version

Characters

Escalus   Prince of Verona

Paris   a count and relative of the Prince

Montague
Capulet } heads of two feuding families

An Old Man   Capulet's relative

Romeo   Montague's son

Mercutio   friend to Romeo and relative of the Prince

Benvolio   friend to Romeo and Montague's nephew

Tybalt   Lady Capulet's nephew

Friar Lawrence
Friar John } Catholic friars of the Franciscan order

Balthazar   Romeo's servant

Sampson
Gregory
Antony
Potpan } servants in the Capulet household

Peter   servant of Juliet's nurse

Abraham   servant of Montague

An Apothecary

Three Musicians

Page to Paris; another Page

Officer

Lady Montague   Montague's wife

Lady Capulet   Capulet's wife

Juliet   Capulet's daughter

Nurse to Juliet

Citizens of Verona; Relatives of both houses; Maskers, Guards, Watchmen, and Attendants

Chorus   announcer

All the World's a Stage Introduction

Under the summer sun in Verona (an Italian city) two families battle in the streets. The grudge is older than most of the people who are doing the fighting. The conflict has become very intense and bitter.

Within this violent place, two teenagers meet and first love blooms. So begins the romance of Shakespeare's *Romeo and Juliet.*

What's in a Name? Characters

Who's who? Most of *Romeo and Juliet*'s characters are tied to the Capulet family or the Montague family. The Montagues include teenage Romeo, his parents (old Montague and his wife), Benvolio, and Abraham and Balthazar (servants). Romeo's friend Mercutio is not related to the Montagues, but he is "on their side."

The Capulet household includes the 14-year-old Juliet, Tybalt (her cousin), Sampson and Gregory (servants), Juliet's parents (Capulet and Lady Capulet), and Juliet's childhood Nurse. The Prince of Verona is named Escalus and he tries to keep peace between the two families. Escalus is related to Mercutio and to a wealthy count named Paris. Another character who wants peace is Friar Lawrence, whom we'll meet in Act 2.

Romeo and Juliet also features a strange "character" called the Chorus. In the plays of ancient Greece, the chorus was a group of people that spoke and danced as one. In *Romeo and Juliet,* the Chorus is like one actor who helps us understand what will happen in the play.

COME WHAT MAY Things to Watch For

Shakespeare frequently mixes dreamy images of love with language that is much more sexual. Often this sexual language includes off-color humor and puns. Such humor can make Shakespeare's tragedy a very funny play. It also shows how ideal love can be brought down to earth.

Shakespeare's audience would have understood jokes about true love and sex. At that time, lovestruck poets wrote about cruelly beautiful and virtuous women. In these poems, the women usually rejected the poet's love. And the poor poet had to find some way to go on living. The language of such love poetry was often exaggerated and artificial.

Some of *Romeo and Juliet*'s most beautiful passages find ways to bridge these extremes. Watch for how Shakespeare explores what is real in romantic love and what is the dreamy stereotype version of passion.

All Our Yesterdays **Historical and Social Context**

Love was one thing, but marriage was another. Shakespeare's audience understood that marriage did not always need love. Men and women worked within a different set of rules and expectations. On the OK list you might find this rule: It is acceptable to marry to increase (or protect) one's wealth and status. On the other list you might find: It is not acceptable to marry only for love. Rich parents from two different families often set up marriages. This type of arranged marriage created peace and wealth between the two families. Young people were expected to follow their parents' wishes and orders, even when they were forced to marry someone they didn't like.

The Play's the Thing **Staging**

Listen up! The speech by the Chorus that introduces the play is called a prologue. It prepares the audience by providing clues and details about the plot and background. In *Romeo and Juliet,* the Chorus gives you a clue about the play's original staging and that it will take "two hours." If this is accurate, Shakespeare's actors must have spoken their lines much faster than actors do today!

The Capulets sure knew how to throw a party. They had *maskers* there as a form of fun and goofiness for the adults. Maskers arrived at parties in weird costumes and disguises to dance and talk with the guests. They often gave performances that were intended to flatter the party's host. At the end of Act 1, an important meeting takes place as a result of masking.

My Words Fly Up **Language**

Some people today might be confused and think that a sonnet is some type of old-fashioned hat. In fact, a *sonnet* is a poetic form. Shakespeare's audience would have understood the sound of a sonnet as soon as they heard one. Shakespeare himself was a famous sonnet writer and he even manages to sneak one into his dialogue. See the section where Romeo and Juliet first meet (lines 91–104 of scene 5). There, the rhyming fourteen-line poem that they speak makes up a moving dance of words between the young pair. The Chorus also speaks in sonnets.

When he talks about love, Romeo often uses images that were typical of sonnets. If he lived today, he'd be quoting pop lyrics instead: rhyming "I'm so blue" with "I love you."

Act I

Prologue

Enter **Chorus**

Chorus Two households both alike in dignity,
In fair Verona where we lay our scene
From ancient grudge, break to new mutiny,
Where civil blood makes civil hands unclean:
5   From forth the fatal loins of these two foes,
A pair of star-crossed lovers take their life:
Whose misadventured piteous overthrows,
Doth with their death bury their parents' strife.
The fearful passage of their death-marked love,
10   And the continuance of their parents' rage,
Which but their children's end nought could remove,
Is now the two hours' traffic of our stage.
The which if you with patient ears attend,
What here shall miss, our toil shall strive to mend.

[*Exit*]

The **Chorus** *enters.*

Chorus Our play takes place in beautiful Verona. Two families, both of the same high rank, have recently started battling again over an ancient grudge. Citizens' hands have been stained with the blood of their fellow townspeople in this civil strife. From these enemy families, a son and a daughter are destined to fall in love, sharing an unfortunate fate. Their tragic deaths bring their parents' fighting to an end. Our two-hour play will tell the sad story of their fatal love and of their parents' bitter feuding, which only the young people's deaths could end.

[*The* **Chorus** *exits*]

Act I

Scene I

Enter **Sampson** *and* **Gregory** *with swords and bucklers of the house of Capulet*

Sampson Gregory, on my word we'll not carry coals.

Gregory No, for then we should be colliers.

Sampson I mean, and we be in choler, we'll draw.

Gregory Ay while you live, draw your neck out of collar.

5 **Sampson** I strike quickly being moved.

Gregory But thou art not quickly moved to strike.

Sampson A dog of the house of Montague moves me.

Gregory To move is to stir, and to be valiant is to stand: therefore if thou art moved, thou runn'st away.

10 **Sampson** A dog of that house shall move me to stand: I will take the wall of any man or maid of Montague's.

Gregory That shows thee a weak slave, for the weakest goes to the wall.

Sampson 'Tis true, and therefore women being the weaker
15 vessels are ever thrust to the wall; therefore I will push Montague's men from the wall and thrust his maids to the wall.

Two servants of the Capulet family, **Sampson** *and* **Gregory,**
enter the stage. They carry swords and shields.

Sampson   I tell you, Gregory, we won't eat dirt.

Gregory   No, because then we'd be like coal miners.

Sampson   What I mean is, if they make us hot under the collar, we'll draw our swords.

Gregory   Yes, but keep your neck out of the collar of a noose.

Sampson   I strike quickly when I get angry.

Gregory   But you don't get angry easily.

Sampson   But those Montague dogs make me angry.

Gregory   To get angry means you get moving. To be courageous means you hold your ground. So if you get moving, you're running away!

Sampson   A Montague dog will get me moving to stand my ground! I won't step aside for any Montague man or maid.

Gregory   That shows what a weak character you are, since the weakest always back up against the wall.

Sampson   That's true. That's why women, being weak, are always backed against the wall. So I'll shove Montague's men out into the street and push his maids against the wall.

Gregory The quarrel is between our masters, and us their men.

20 **Sampson** 'Tis all one. I will show myself a tyrant; when I have fought with the men, I will be civil with the maids, I will cut off their heads.

Gregory The heads of the maids?

Sampson Ay, the heads of the maids, or their maidenheads;
25   take it in what sense thou wilt.

Gregory They must take it in sense that feel it.

Sampson Me they shall feel while I am able to stand, and 'tis known I am a pretty piece of flesh.

Gregory 'Tis well thou are not fish; if thou hadst, thou hadst
30   been poor John: draw thy tool, here comes two of the house of Montagues.

[*Enter two other Servingmen,* **Abraham** *and* **Balthazar**]

Sampson My naked weapon is out: quarrel, I will back thee.

Gregory How, turn thy back and run?

Sampson Fear me not.

35 **Gregory** No marry; I fear thee.

Sampson Let us take the law of our sides; let them begin.

Gregory I will frown as I pass by, and let them take it as they list.

Sampson Nay, as they dare. I will bite my thumb at them,
40   which is disgrace to them if they bear it.

Gregory The quarrel is just between our masters, and between us, our masters' men.

Sampson It makes no difference to me. I'll be a real scoundrel. After I've fought all the men, I'll be polite to the maids—I'll cut off their heads.

Gregory The heads of the maids?

Sampson Yes, the heads of the maids, or their maidenheads—that is, their virginity! Take it in whatever sense you want to.

Gregory If they sense it, they should feel it!

Sampson They'll feel me as long as I'm able to stand. It's well known that I'm a nice piece of flesh.

Gregory It's good you're not a fish. If you were, you'd be a poor catch! Draw your sword. Here come two men from the house of Montague.

[*Two servants,* **Abraham** *and* **Balthazar,** *enter*]

Sampson My sword is out. Start a quarrel with them. I'll back you.

Gregory How do you mean "back me"? Do you mean turn your back and run?

Sampson Don't worry about me!

Gregory Of course not. I'm not worried about *you*!

Sampson Let's make sure the law is on our side. Let them start something.

Gregory I'll give them a dirty look when I walk by. Let them take it however they want to.

Sampson Or how they dare to. I'll give them the finger. They'll be disgraced if they don't do something about that.

Abraham Do you bite your thumb at us sir?

Sampson I do bite my thumb sir.

Abraham Do you bite your thumb at us sir?

Sampson Is the law of our side if I say ay?

45 **Gregory** No.

Sampson No sir, I do not bite my thumb at you sir, but I bite
my thumb sir.

Gregory Do you quarrel sir?

Abraham Quarrel sir, no sir.

50 **Sampson** But if you do sir, I am for you; I serve as good a
man as you.

Abraham No better.

Sampson Well sir.

[*Enter* **Benvolio**]

Gregory Say better: here comes one of my master's kinsmen.

55 **Sampson** Yes, better sir.

Abraham You lie.

Sampson Draw if you be men. Gregory, remember thy
washing blow.

[*They fight*]

Benvolio Part fools.
60   Put up your swords, you know not what you do.

[*Enter* **Tybalt**]

Abraham   Did you give us the finger, sir?

Sampson   I gave the finger.

Abraham   Did you give *us* the finger, sir?

Sampson   [*to* **Gregory**]   Is the law on our side if I say yes?

Gregory   No.

Sampson   No sir, I did not give *you* the finger, sir, but I did give the finger.

Gregory   Do you want to start something, sir?

Abraham   Start something, sir? No, sir.

Sampson   Well, if you do, sir, I'm ready. My master is as good as yours.

Abraham   No better?

Sampson   Well sir . . .

[**Benvolio,** *a Montague, enters*]

Gregory   Say "better." Here comes one of our master's relatives. [*He means* **Tybalt,** *who is about to enter*]

Sampson   Yes, better, sir.

Abraham   You're a liar!

Sampson   Draw your swords, if you're man enough. Gregory, don't forget your slashing stroke!

[*They fight*]

Benvolio   Stop it, you fools. Put away your swords. You don't know what you're doing.

[**Tybalt,** *a Capulet, enters*]

Tybalt What, art thou drawn among these hartless hinds?
Turn thee Benvolio, look upon thy death.

Benvolio I do but keep the peace; put up thy sword,
Or manage it to part these men with me.

65 **Tybalt** What, drawn and talk of peace? I hate the word
As I hate hell, all Montagues, and thee.
Have at thee coward!

[*They fight*]

[*Enter three or four* **Citizens** *with clubs or partisans*]

Officer Clubs, bills and partisans, strike, beat them down!

Citizens Down with the Capulets, down with the Montagues!

[*Enter old* **Capulet** *and* **Lady Capulet**]

70 **Capulet** What noise is this? Give me my long sword, ho!

Lady Capulet A crutch, a crutch; why call you for a sword?

Capulet My sword I say! Old Montague is come,
And flourishes his blade in spite of me.

[*Enter old* **Montague** *and* **Lady Montague**]

Montague Thou villain Capulet: hold me not, let me go.

75 **Lady Montague** Thou shalt not stir one foot to seek a foe.

[*Enter* **Prince Escalus** *with his train*]

Tybalt   What! Are you fighting with mere servants, these timid deer? Turn around, Benvolio. Face your death!

Benvolio   I'm just trying to keep the peace. Put away your sword. Or use it to help me separate these men.

Tybalt   What! Talking about peace with your sword drawn? I hate the word "peace" as I hate hell, and all the Montagues, and you! Come on, coward!

[*They fight*]

[*Three or four* **Citizens** *join the fight*]

Officer   Clubs, axes, spears! Stop! Put them down!

Citizens   Down with the Capulets! Down with the Montagues!

[*Old* **Capulet** *and* **Lady Capulet** *enter*]

Capulet   What's all the noise? Give me my long sword, you there!

Lady Capulet   [*referring to her husband's old age*]   A crutch, you mean! A crutch! Why are you asking for a sword?

Capulet   My sword, I said. Old Montague is coming. He's waving his sword to anger me.

[*Old* **Montague** *and* **Lady Montague** *enter*]

Montague   You villain, Capulet! Don't try to stop me! Let me go!

Lady Montague   You shall not make one single step toward the enemy.

[**Prince Escalus** *and his men enter*]

current

Prince   Rebellious subjects, enemies to peace,
Profaners of this neighbour-stained steel –
Will they not hear? What ho, you men, you beasts
That quench the fire of your pernicious rage
80   With purple fountains issuing from your veins:
On pain of torture, from those bloody hands,
Throw your mistempered weapons to the ground,
And hear the sentence of your moved Prince.
Three civil brawls bred of an airy word,
85   By thee old Capulet and Montague,
Have thrice disturbed the quiet of our streets,
And made Verona's ancient citizens
Cast by their grave beseeming ornaments
To wield old partisans, in hands as old,
90   Cankered with peace, to part your cankered hate.
If ever you disturb our streets again
Your lives shall pay the forfeit of the peace.
For this time all the rest depart away;
You, Capulet, shall go along with me,
95   And Montague, come you this afternoon,
To know our farther pleasure in this case,
To old Freetown, our common judgement-place.
Once more, on pain of death, all men depart.

[*Exeunt all but* **Montague, Lady Montague** *and* **Benvolio**]

Montague   Who set this ancient quarrel new abroach?
100   Speak, nephew, were you by when it began?

Benvolio   Here were the servants of your adversary
And yours, close fighting ere I did approach.
I drew to part them; in the instant came
The fiery Tybalt, with his sword prepared,
105   Which, as he breathed defiance to my ears
He swung about his head and cut the winds,

Prince You rebels! Enemies of peace! You stain your swords with your neighbors' blood! [*The fighting continues*] Can't you hear? Hey, you men there! You beasts that put out the fire of your anger with the blood from your veins. On pain of torture, drop those weapons from your bloody hands. Now listen to the judgment of your angry Prince. Three fights have occurred because of a few words from you, old Capulet, and from you, Montague, disturbing our quiet streets. Verona's oldest citizens have put aside their dignified manner and taken up old rusted weapons, in hands just as old and rusty with peace, to break up your cancerous fight. If you ever disturb the peace of our town again, you will pay with your lives. For now, let the crowd break up. You, Capulet, will go with me, and you, Montague, will come to see me this afternoon at our court at old Freetown, to learn what else I have decided in this matter. Once again—on pain of death— everyone disperse!

[*Everyone but* **Montague, Lady Montague,** *and* **Benvolio** *exits*]

Montague Who started up this quarrel again? Speak, nephew; were you here when it began?

Benvolio Your enemy's servants and your servants were fighting hand to hand before I arrived. I drew my sword to stop them, but just then that fiery-tempered Tybalt arrived. He had his sword out and was shouting insults at me, swinging the sword around his head. His sword swished in the air, but I wasn't hurt, and the sword seemed to hiss in

Who nothing hurt withal, hissed him in scorn.
While we were interchanging thrusts and blows
Came more and more, and fought on part and part,
110 Till the Prince came, who parted either part.

Lady Montague O where is Romeo, saw you him today?
Right glad I am he was not at this fray.

Benvolio Madam, an hour before the worshipped sun
Peered forth the golden window of the east
115 A troubled mind drive me to walk abroad,
Where underneath the grove of sycamore
That westward rooteth from this city side,
So early walking did I see your son.
Towards him I made, but he was ware of me,
120 And stole into the covert of the wood.
I, measuring his affections by my own,
Which then most sought, where most might not be found,
Being one too many by my weary self,
Pursued my humour, not pursuing his,
125 And gladly shunned who gladly fled from me.

Montague Many a morning hath he there been seen,
With tears augmenting the fresh morning's dew,
Adding to clouds more clouds with his deep sighs;
But all so soon as the all-cheering sun
130 Should in the farthest east begin to draw
The shady curtains from Aurora's bed,
Away from light steals home my heavy son
And private in his chamber pens himself,
Shuts up his windows, locks fair daylight out
135 And makes himself an artificial night.
Black and portentous must this humour prove
Unless good counsel may the cause remove.

Benvolio My noble uncle, do you know the cause?

Montague I neither know it nor can learn of him.

scorn. While we were exchanging thrusts and blows, others came and joined in, fighting one-on-one, until the Prince came and stopped them.

Lady Montague Where is Romeo? Did you see him today? I'm very glad he wasn't in this fight.

Benvolio Madam, an hour before the sun appeared at its golden window in the east, my mind was troubled and I went for a walk. In the grove of sycamore trees that grows on the west side of the city, I saw your son taking an early morning walk. I started toward him, but he saw me and hid in the woods. I believed he felt as I did then. What I wanted most was to be where there were the fewest people. My own weary self was one too many. I followed my feelings and didn't follow him. I was happy to avoid him, just as he was happy to avoid me.

Montague He's been seen there many a morning, his tears adding to the new morning's dew, the clouds formed by his deep sighs adding to the clouds that already exist. But as soon as the cheery sun begins to rise in the east, pushing back the curtains of night, my gloomy son comes home to avoid the light. He locks himself in his room, closes the shutters on his windows to lock out the daylight, makes an artificial night for himself. This mood of his will prove black and ominous, unless good advice can remove the reason for it.

Benvolio My noble uncle, do you know the reason?

Montague I don't know it, and I can't find it out from him.

140   **Benvolio** Have you importuned him by any means?

Montague Both by myself and many other friends.
But he, his own affections' counsellor,
Is to himself – I will not say how true –
But to himself so secret and so close,
145   So far from sounding and discovery,
As is the bud bit with an envious worm
Ere he can spread his sweet leaves to the air
Or dedicate his beauty to the sun.
Could we but learn from whence his sorrows grow,
150   We would as willingly give cure as know.

[*Enter* **Romeo**]

Benvolio See where he comes. So please you step aside;
I'll know his grievance or be much denied.

Montague I would thou wert so happy by thy stay
To hear true shrift. Come, madam, let's away.

[*Exeunt* **Montague** *and* **Lady Montague**]

155   **Benvolio** Good morrow, cousin.

Romeo   Is the day so young?

Benvolio But new struck nine.

Romeo   Ay me, sad hours seem long.
Was that my father that went hence so fast?

160   **Benvolio** It was. What sadness lengthens Romeo's hours?

Romeo Not having that which, having, makes them short.

Benvolio In love?

Romeo Out.

Benvolio Of love?

Benvolio Have you questioned him in any way?

Montague I have, and many other friends have as well. But he's so withdrawn, he keeps his thoughts to himself. He's so secretive and so closed, so far from letting others understand him. He's like a flower bud that's being eaten by a spiteful worm before it can spread its petals open to the air or show its beauty to the sun. If we could find out why he's so sad, we would just as willingly find a cure.

[**Romeo** *enters*]

Benvolio Look, he's coming. If you please, step aside. I'll find out what's bothering him, unless he just refuses to tell me.

Montague I hope your efforts are successful. Come madam, let's go.

[**Montague** *and* **Lady Montague** *exit*]

Benvolio Good morning, cousin.

Romeo Is the day that young?

Benvolio The clock's just struck nine.

Romeo Ah me! The hours seem long when you're sad. Was that my father who left so quickly?

Benvolio It was. What sadness makes time seem so long for you, Romeo?

Romeo Not having that something which, if I had it, would make time seem short.

Benvolio In love?

Romeo Out.

Benvolio Of love?

165 **Romeo** Out of her favour where I am in love.

Benvolio Alas that love so gentle in his view
Should be so tyrannous and rough in proof.

Romeo Alas that love whose view is muffled still
Should without eyes see pathways to his will.
170 Where shall we dine? O me! What fray was here?
Yet tell me not, for I have heard it all.
Here's much to do with hate, but more with love.
Why then, O brawling love, O loving hate,
O anything of nothing first create!
175 O heavy lightness, serious vanity,
Misshapen chaos of well-seeming forms!
Feather of lead, bright smoke, cold fire, sick health,
Still-waking sleep that is not what it is!
This love feel I that feel no love in this.
180 Dost thou not laugh?

Benvolio   No coz, I rather weep.

Romeo Good heart, at what?

Benvolio   At thy good heart's oppression.

Romeo Why such is love's transgression.
185 Griefs of mine own lie heavy in my breast,
Which thou wilt propagate to have it pressed
With more of thine. This love that thou hast shown
Doth add more grief to too much of mine own.
Love is a smoke made with the fume of sighs;
190 Being purged, a fire sparkling in lovers' eyes;
Being vexed, a sea nourished with lovers' tears;
What is it else? A madness most discreet,
A choking gall, and a preserving sweet.
Farewell, my coz.

195 **Benvolio**   Soft, I will go along;
And if you leave me so, you do me wrong.

Romeo Out of favor with the one I love.

Benvolio Too bad that Cupid, who looks so gentle, should be so harsh and rough in his actual behavior.

Romeo Too bad that Cupid, whose eyes are blindfolded, should see his targets without eyes. Where shall we have dinner? Oh me! What caused the fight? Never mind, don't tell me. I've heard it all. It's a lot about hate, but more about love. Oh brawling love! Oh loving hate! Oh anything that was created out of nothing! Oh heavy lightness! Serious foolishness! Grotesque confusion made of things that appear well formed! Feather of lead, bright smoke, cold fire, sick health, wakeful sleep that is not sleep! I feel this love, but feel no love from her. Do you laugh?

Benvolio No cousin, I'm weeping.

Romeo Dear friend, at what?

Benvolio At your good heart's pain.

Romeo Well, that's how love goes. My own grief, that lies heavy in my heart, will increase if you add your own to it. This love you've shown adds more grief to my already great quantity of it. Love is smoke made from the fumes of sighs. When it burns away, it's a fire sparkling in lovers' eyes. When it's troubled, it's a sea filled with lovers' tears. What else is it? A cautious madness, a bitter potion, a healing sweetness. Goodbye, cousin.

Benvolio Wait, I'll go with you. You do me wrong if you leave me like this.

Romeo   Tut, I have lost myself, I am not here.
This is not Romeo, he's some other where.

Benvolio   Tell me in sadness who is that you love?

200   **Romeo**   What, shall I groan and tell thee?

Benvolio   Groan? Why no, but sadly tell me who.

Romeo   Bid a sick man in sadness make his will?
A word ill-urged to one that is so ill.
In sadness, cousin, I do love a woman.

205   **Benvolio**   I aimed so near when I supposed you loved.

Romeo   A right good markman! And she's fair I love.

Benvolio   A right fair mark, fair coz, is soonest hit.

Romeo   Well, in that hit you miss; she'll not be hit
With Cupid's arrow, she hath Dian's wit,
210   And in strong proof of chastity well armed
From love's weak childish bow she lives unharmed.
She will not stay the siege of loving terms
Nor bid th' encounter of assailing eyes
Nor ope her lap to saint-seducing gold;
215   O she is rich in beauty, only poor
That when she dies, with beauty dies her store.

Benvolio   Then she hath sworn that she will still live chaste?

Romeo   She hath, and in that sparing makes huge waste.
But beauty starved with her severity
220   Cuts beauty off from all posterity.
She is too fair, too wise, wisely too fair,
To merit bliss by making me despair.
She hath forsworn to love, and in that vow
Do I live dead, that live to tell it now.

225   **Benvolio**   Be ruled by me, forget to think of her.

Romeo   Nonsense; I've lost myself. I'm not here with you. This isn't Romeo—he's somewhere else.

Benvolio   Tell me, seriously. Who do you love?

Romeo   What? Should I groan sorrowfully and tell you?

Benvolio   Groan? Why no. But seriously, tell me who it is.

Romeo   Tell a sick man to make his will "seriously"? A poor choice of words to someone who's so sick, who's such a "serious case." Seriously, cousin, I love a woman.

Benvolio   I was aiming at that target when I guessed you were in love.

Romeo   Well, a good marksman! And the woman I love is beautiful!

Benvolio   Well, a target that catches your eye is the easiest to hit!

Romeo   Well, this time you missed the target. She can't be hit with Cupid's arrows. She has the wisdom of the goddess Diana. She defends her virginity with strong armor, and Cupid's weak little bow can't harm her. She resists sweet talk and loving looks. She won't be won even by an amount of gold that would tempt a saint. Oh, she's rich in beauty! But she's poor—only because when she dies, her beauty and fertility will die with her.

Benvolio   Then she has sworn to remain a virgin all her life?

Romeo   She has. And what a huge waste that is! Her beauty will be starved by her severe choice, and her virginity will cut off her beauty from all future generations that might inherit it. She is too beautiful and too wise to win a place in heaven by making me suffer. She has sworn never to love, and because of that vow, I'm in a state of living death, even as I live to talk about it now.

Benvolio   Listen to me. Forget about her.

Romeo O teach me how I should forget to think.

Benvolio By giving liberty unto thine eyes:
Examine other beauties.

Romeo   'Tis the way.
230   To call hers, exquisite, in question more.
These happy masks that kiss fair ladies' brows,
Being black, puts us in mind they hide the fair.
He that is strucken blind cannot forget
The precious treasure of his eyesight lost.
235   Show me a mistress that is passing fair;
What doth her beauty serve but as a note
Where I may read who passed that passing fair?
Farewell, thou canst not teach me to forget.

Benvolio I'll pay that doctrine or else die in debt.

[*Exeunt*]

Romeo   Teach me how to forget.

Benvolio   By allowing your eyes to wander. Look around at other beautiful young women.

Romeo   That's a sure way to make her beauty seem even more exquisite. These dark veils that beautiful ladies wear over their faces make us think about the beauty that the veils hide. A man who has gone blind can't forget the precious treasure of his lost eyesight. Show me a woman who is beautiful. What does her beauty do but remind me of one who is even more beautiful? Goodbye. You can't teach me to forget.

Benvolio   I'll teach you that lesson, or else fail as your friend.

[**Romeo** *and* **Benvolio** *exit*]

Act I

Scene II

Enter **Capulet, County Paris** *and the* **Clown, Capulet's** *servant*

Capulet But Montague is bound as well as I,
In penalty alike, and 'tis not hard I think
For men so old as we to keep the peace.

Paris Of honourable reckoning are you both,
5 And pity 'tis you lived at odds so long.
But now my lord, what say you to my suit?

Capulet But saying o'er what I have said before.
My child is yet a stranger in the world,
She hath not seen the change of fourteen years.
10 Let two more summers wither in their pride
Ere we may think her ripe to be a bride.

Paris Younger than she are happy mothers made.

Capulet And too soon marred are those so early made.
Earth hath swallowed all my hopes but she;
15 She is the hopeful lady of my earth.
But woo her, gentle Paris, get her heart,
My will to her consent is but a part,
And she agreed, within her scope of choice
Lies my consent and fair according voice.
20 This night I hold an old accustomed feast
Whereto I have invited many a guest
Such as I love, and you among the store:
One more, most welcome, makes my number more.

46

Capulet, Count Paris, *and the* **Clown, Capulet's** *servant, enter.*

Capulet   But Montague is bound by the ruling just as I am, with the same penalty. I don't think it will be hard for men as old as us to keep the peace.

Paris   You both have reputations for honor. It's a pity you have been at odds with each other for so long. But now, my lord, what do you say about my suit to marry your daughter?

Capulet   I'll say again what I've said before. My child is very young; she's still a stranger to this world. She hasn't yet turned fourteen. Let two more years pass before we think she's ready to be a bride.

Paris   Girls younger than she are happy mothers.

Capulet   And those who are made mothers so early are soon ruined. The grave has swallowed up all my children but her. She is the hope of my world. But woo her, gentle Paris; win her heart. My wishes are not as important as her feelings. If she agrees, then I'll grant my consent freely. Tonight I'm holding a feast, one that I customarily hold. I have invited many good friends, and you are invited as well. You will be a most welcome addition.

At my poor house look to behold this night
25 Earth-treading stars that make dark heaven light.
Such comfort as do lusty young men feel
When well-apparelled April on the heel
Of limping winter treads, even such delight
Among fresh female buds shall you this night
30 Inherit at my house. Hear all, all see,
And like her most whose merit most shall be;
Which, on more view of many, mine, being one,
May stand in number, though in reckoning none.
Come, go with me.

[*To the* **Clown,** *giving him a paper*]

35   Go sirrah, trudge about
Through fair Verona, find those persons out
Whose names are written there, and to them say,
My house and welcome on their pleasure stay.

[*Exeunt* **Capulet** *and* **Paris**]

Clown   Find them out whose names are written here! It is
40   written that the shoemaker should meddle with his yard, and
the tailor with his last, the fisher with his pencil, and the
painter with his nets, but I am sent to find those persons
whose names are here writ, and can never find what names
the writing person hath here writ. I must to the learned.
45 ——In good time!

[*Enter* **Benvolio** *and* **Romeo**]

Benvolio   Tut man, one fire burns out another's burning,
One pain is lessened by another's anguish;
Turn giddy, and be holp by backward turning.
One desperate grief cures with another's languish;
50 Take thou some new infection to thy eye
And the rank poison of the old will die.

Tonight at my humble house, plan to see women as beautiful as stars that light up the dark heavens and that have come down to earth. Tonight, the sight of these fresh female flower buds will give you as much pleasure as young men feel when April appears on the heels of a tired winter, wearing her best spring dress. Hear them all, see them all. Then like the best girl the most. After you see so many, my daughter, being one of them, may turn out to be your number one. (Although one isn't considered a number!) Now, come with me.

[**Capulet** *gives a paper to the* **Clown**]

You there, servant, go around beautiful Verona and find those people whose names are written on this list. Tell them I would welcome the pleasure of their company at my house.

[**Capulet** *and* **Paris** *exit*]

Clown   Find those people whose names are written here? They say that the shoemaker should keep to his yardstick, the tailor to his shoe form, the fisherman to his pencil, and the painter to his nets. But I'm sent to find people whose names are written here, even though I can't read what names the writer wrote down. I must ask someone who's learned to read. Ah, good timing!

[**Benvolio** *and* **Romeo** *enter*]

Benvolio   [*to* **Romeo**] Look, man! One fire burns out another fire. One pain is lessened by another pain. When you're dizzy from turning, you can fix it by turning in reverse. A desperate grief is cured by another grief. So with love. If you get a new infection in your sight, the poison of the old infection will die.

Romeo   Your plantain leaf is excellent for that.

Benvolio   For what, I pray thee?

Romeo   For your broken shin.

55 **Benvolio**   Why, Romeo, art thou mad?

Romeo   Not mad, but bound more than a madman is:
    Shut up in prison, kept without my food,
    Whipped and tormented and – good e'en, good fellow.

Clown   God gi' good e'en; I pray, sir, can you read?

60 **Romeo**   Ay, mine own fortune in my misery.

Clown   Perhaps you have learned it without book. But I pray
    can you read anything you see?

Romeo   Ay, if I know the letters and the language.

Clown   Ye say honestly; rest you merry.

65 **Romeo**   Stay, fellow, I can read. [*He reads the list*]

    'Signor Martino and his wife and daughters;
    County Anselm and his beauteous sisters;
    The lady widow of Utruvio;
    Signor Placentio and his lovely nieces;
70 Mercutio and his brother Valentine;
    Mine uncle Capulet, his wife and daughters;
    My fair niece Rosaline and Livia;
    Signor Valentio and his cousin Tybalt;
    Lucio and the lively Helena.'

75   A fair assembly. Whither should they come?

Clown   Up.

Romeo The plantain leaf is excellent for that.

Benvolio For what?

Romeo For your broken shin.

Benvolio Romeo! Have you gone mad?

Romeo No, I'm not mad. But I'm tied up more tightly than a madman is. I'm shut up in prison, kept without food, whipped and tormented, and—Good afternoon, good fellow!

Clown And God give you a good afternoon. Tell me, sir, can you read?

Romeo Yes, I can read my own miserable future in the misery I suffer now.

Clown Perhaps you've learned that without a book. But, tell me, can you read anything you see?

Romeo Yes, if I know the alphabet and language in which it's written.

Clown That's honestly said. Have a good day.

Romeo Wait, man. I can read. [*He reads the list*]

"Signor Martino and his wife and daughters;
Count Anselm and his beautiful sisters;
The lady widow of Utruvio;
Signor Placentio and his lovely nieces;
Mercutio and his brother Valentine;
My uncle Capulet, his wife and daughters;
My fair niece Rosaline and Livia;
Signor Valentio and his cousin Tybalt;
Lucio and the lively Helena."

A pleasant group. Where shall they go?

Clown Up.

Romeo Whither to supper?

Clown To our house.

Romeo Whose house?

80 **Clown** My master's.

Romeo Indeed, I should have asked you that before.

Clown Now I'll tell you without asking. My master is the great
rich Capulet, and if you be not of the house of Montagues I
pray come and crush a cup of wine. Rest you merry.

[*Exit*]

85 **Benvolio** At this same ancient feast of Capulet's
Sups the fair Rosaline, whom thou so loves,
With all the admired beauties of Verona.
Go thither, and with unattainted eye
Compare her face with some that I shall show,
90   And I will make thee think thy swan a crow.

Romeo When the devout religion of mine eye
Maintains such falsehood, then turn tears to fires;
And those who, often drowned, could never die,
Transparent heretics, be burnt for liars.
95   One fairer than my love! The all-seeing sun
Ne'er saw her match, since first the world begun.

Benvolio Tut, you saw her fair none else being by,
Herself poised with herself in either eye;
But in that crystal scales let there be weighed
100   Your lady's love against some other maid
That I will show you shining at this feast,
And she shall scant show well that now seems best.

Romeo I'll go along, no such sight to be shown,
But to rejoice in splendour of mine own.

[*Exeunt*]

Romeo Up? To supper?

Clown To our house.

Romeo Whose house?

Clown My master's.

Romeo Yes, I should have asked you that before!

Clown Now I'll tell you without asking. My master is the great rich Capulet. And if you aren't from the house of Montague, then please come and drink a cup of wine. Have a good day!

[*The* **Clown** *exits*]

Benvolio The beautiful Rosaline whom you love so much will dine at this feast of Capulet's, along with all the most beautiful women in Verona. Go to the feast, and with an objective eye, compare her face with some others that I'll show you. I'll make you think that your swan is really a crow!

Romeo If my religiously faithful eye ever accepts such a lie, then I hope my tears turn to fire. And just like heretics who are drowned first to test them, may my eyes be burnt as liars. Someone more beautiful than my love? The all-seeing sun has never seen anyone as beautiful since the world first began!

Benvolio Look, you saw her as beautiful because there was no one else with whom to compare her. She alone was balanced against herself in both of your eyes. But use the same eyes, like crystal scales, to weigh your lady against some other gorgeous girl that I'll show you at this feast. The girl you love will seem barely passable, even though now she seems like the best.

Romeo I'll go—not to see what you have to show, but to rejoice in the splendor of Rosaline.

[**Romeo** *and* **Benvolio** *exit*]

Act I

Scene III

Capulet's house. Enter **Lady Capulet** *and* **Nurse**

Lady Capulet Nurse, where's my daughter? Call her forth to
me.

Nurse Now by my maidenhead at twelve year old,
I bade her come. What, lamb! What, ladybird!
God forbid. Where's this girl? What, Juliet!

[*Enter* **Juliet**]

Juliet How now, who calls?

Nurse   Your mother.

Juliet Madam, I am here, what is your will?

Lady Capulet This is the matter. Nurse, give leave awhile,
We must talk in secret. Nurse, come back again,
I have remembered me, thou's hear our counsel.
Thou knowest my daughter's of a pretty age.

Nurse Faith, I can tell her age unto an hour.

Lady Capulet She's not fourteen.

Nurse   I'll lay fourteen of my teeth,
And yet, to my teen be it spoken, I have but four,
She's not fourteen. How long is it now to
Lammas-tide?

Capulet's house. **Lady Capulet** *and the* **Nurse** *enter.*

Lady Capulet Nurse, where's my daughter? Call her to me.

Nurse Now by my virginity at twelve years old, I told her to come! Yoo-hoo, lamb! Yoo-hoo, ladybird! God forbid that something's wrong! Where is that girl? Yoo-hoo, Juliet!

[**Juliet** *enters*]

Juliet What is it? Who's calling?

Nurse Your mother.

Juliet Madam, here I am. What do you wish?

Lady Capulet This is what. Nurse, leave us a while; we must talk privately. Nurse, come back again. I've thought of something else. You'll hear our conversation. You know my daughter is of a pretty age.

Nurse Certainly, I can tell her age to the hour.

Lady Capulet She's not yet fourteen.

Nurse I'll bet fourteen of my teeth—but the sad truth is, I have only four—she's not fourteen. How long is it now to Lammas Day, August 1?

Lady Capulet   A fortnight and odd days.

20 **Nurse** Even or odd, of all days in the year,
        Come Lammas Eve at night shall she be fourteen.
        Susan and she – God rest all Christian souls –
        Were of an age. Well, Susan is with God:
        She was too good for me. But as I said,
25   On Lammas Eve at night shall she be fourteen.
        That shall she. Marry, I remember it well.
        'Tis since the earthquake now eleven years,
        And she was weaned – I never shall forget it –
        Of all the days of the year upon that day.
30   For I had then laid wormwood to my dug,
        Sitting in the sun under the dovehouse wall.
        My lord and you were then at Mantua –
        Nay I do bear a brain. But as I said,
        When it did taste the wormwood on the nipple
35   Of my dug and felt it bitter, pretty fool,
        To see it tetchy and fall out with the dug.
        Shake! quoth the dovehouse. 'Twas no need, I trow,
        To bid me trudge.
        And since that time it is eleven years.
40   For then she could stand high-lone, nay, by th' rood,
        She could have run and waddled all about;
        For even the day before she broke her brow,
        And then my husband, God be with his soul,
        'A was a merry man, took up the child,
45   'Yea', quoth he, 'dost thou fall upon thy face?
        Thou wilt fall backward when thou hast more wit,
        Wilt thou not, Jule?' And by my holidame,
        The pretty wretch left crying and said, 'Ay'.
        To see now how a jest shall come about.
50   I warrant, and I should live a thousand years
        I never should forget it. 'Wilt thou not, Jule?' quoth he,
        And, pretty fool, it stinted, and said, 'Ay'.

Lady Capulet Enough of this, I pray thee, hold thy peace.

Lady Capulet Two weeks and some-odd days.

Nurse Even or odd, of all the days in the year, on the night of Lammas Eve, she'll be fourteen. Susan and she—God rest all Christian souls—were the same age. Well, Susan is with God; she was too good for me. But as I said, on Lammas Eve night, she'll be fourteen. That she shall. Yes indeed, I remember it well. It's been eleven years now since the earthquake. And she was weaned—I shall never forget it—of all the days of the year on that same day. I had placed some wormwood on my breast, and was sitting in the sun under the dovehouse wall. You and the master were in Mantua— my, I do have a good memory. But as I said, when she tasted the wormwood on my nipple and it was bitter, the pretty little one, she became irritable and refused the breast. Then the dovehouse began to shake. There was no need, believe me, to tell me to move. And it's been eleven years since then. She could stand alone then. In fact, by the Holy Cross, she could run and toddle about. The day before that, she bumped her forehead. And then my husband (God be with his soul, he was a jolly man) picked her up. "Oh," he said, "did you fall on your face? You'll fall on your back when you learn a little more, won't you, Jule?" And by my holy namesake, the pretty little thing stopped crying and said, "Yes!" Imagine how a joke could be so true! I swear, if I live a thousand years, I'll never forget it. "Won't you, Jule?" he said, and the pretty little one stopped crying and said "Yes!"

Lady Capulet That's enough of this. Please, be quiet.

Nurse Yes, madam, yet I cannot choose but laugh
55   To think it should leave crying and say 'Ay'.
    And yet I warrant it had upon its brow
    A bump as big as a young cockerel's stone,
    A perilous knock, and it cried bitterly.
    'Yea', quoth my husband, 'fall'st upon thy face?
60   Thou wilt fall backward when thou comest to age,
    Wilt thou not, Jule?' It stinted, and said 'Ay'.

Juliet And stint thou too, I pray thee, Nurse, say I.

Nurse Peace, I have done. God mark thee to his grace,
    Thou wast the prettiest babe that e'er I nursed.
65   And I might live to see thee married once,
    I have my wish.

Lady Capulet Marry, that marry is the very theme
    I came to talk of. Tell me, daughter Juliet,
    How stands your dispositions to be married?

70 **Juliet** It is an honour that I dream not of.

Nurse An honour! Were not I thine only nurse
    I would say thou hadst sucked wisdom from thy teat.

Lady Capulet Well, think of marriage now. Younger
        than you
75   Here in Verona, ladies of esteem,
    Are made already mothers. By my count
    I was your mother much upon these years
    That you are now a maid. Thus then in brief:
    The valiant Paris seeks you for his love.

80 **Nurse** A man, young lady! Lady, such a man
    As all the world – why, he's a man of wax.

Lady Capulet Verona's summer hath not such a flower.

Nurse Nay, he's a flower, in faith a very flower.

Nurse Yes, madam, but I can't help but laugh to think how she stopped crying and said, "Yes!" And I swear, she had a bump on her head as big as a young rooster's testicles, a terrible bump, and she cried bitterly. "Oh," said my husband, "did you fall on your face? You'll fall on your back when you get to be old enough, won't you, Jule?" She stopped crying and said "Yes!"

Juliet And you stop too, please Nurse!

Nurse Okay, I'm finished. God bless you. You were the prettiest babe I've ever nursed. And if I live to see you married, I'll have my wish.

Lady Capulet By Mary, getting married is the very thing I came to talk about. Tell me, daughter Juliet, what are your feelings about getting married?

Juliet It's an honor that I don't even dream of.

Nurse An honor! If I hadn't been your only nurse, I'd say that you had sucked wisdom from the breast.

Lady Capulet Well, think of marriage now. Younger ladies than you, high-born ladies, are already mothers here in Verona. By my count, I was your mother at just about the age that you are now. So, to be brief—the noble Paris wishes you for his bride.

Nurse A man, young lady! Lady, such a man as the whole world— why he's a man of such perfection, as if he were made of wax!

Lady Capulet You won't find such a flower even in Verona's summer.

Nurse Yes, he's a flower. In truth, a flower!

Lady Capulet What say you, can you love the gentleman?
85   This night you shall behold him at our feast;
     Read o'er the volume of young Paris' face
     And find delight writ there with beauty's pen.
     Examine every married lineament
     And see how one another lends content;
90   And what obscured in this fair volume lies,
     Find written in the margent of his eyes.
     This precious book of love, this unbound lover,
     To beautify him only lacks a cover.
     The fish lives in the sea; and 'tis much pride
95   For fair without the fair within to hide.
     That book in many's eyes doth share the glory
     That in gold clasps locks in the golden story.
     So shall you share all that he doth possess,
     By having him, making yourself no less.

100 **Nurse** No less, nay bigger. Women grow by men.

Lady Capulet Speak briefly, can you like of Paris' love?

Juliet I'll look to like, if looking liking move,
     But no more deep will I endart mine eye
     Than your consent gives strength to make it fly.

[*Enter a* **Servingman**]

105 **Servingman** Madam, the guests are come, supper served up,
you called, my young lady asked for, the Nurse cursed in
the pantry, and everything in extremity. I must hence to wait,
I beseech you follow straight.

[*Exit*]

Lady Capulet We follow thee. Juliet, the County stays.

110 **Nurse** Go, girl, seek happy nights to happy days.

[*Exeunt*]

Lady Capulet What do you say? Can you love the gentleman? Tonight you'll see him at our feast. Examine his face closely, as if it were a book. You'll find that the contents are delightfully attractive. Examine every harmonious feature. See how each one tells part of the story. If anything is unclear in this lovely book, look into his eyes for the notes that explain. This precious book of love, this love that's still unbound, has everything except a cover. Just as a fish is surrounded by the sea, so a beautiful cover surrounds the beauty inside, and so a beautiful wife makes a suitable fit to go with a handsome man. Many people think that when gold clasps lock the cover of a beautiful story, the book's cover shares the beauty of the tale. In the same way, you'll share all his qualities by marrying him. You won't be the less for it.

Nurse Not less? No—bigger. Women grow larger when they're made pregnant by men.

Lady Capulet Tell me briefly: Can you like the thought of Paris's love?

Juliet If looking at him makes me like him, then I shall. But I won't look any deeper than you give me permission to.

[*A* **Servant** *enters*]

Servant Madam, the guests are here; supper is served. They're calling for you and asking for the young lady. The Nurse is being cursed in the pantry, and everything's in confusion. I must go to wait on the tables. Please come right away.

[*The* **Servant** *exits*]

Lady Capulet We'll follow you. Juliet, the Count is waiting.

Nurse Go on, girl. Look for happy nights, and they'll make happy days.

[*They exit*]

Act I

Scene IV

A street. Enter **Romeo, Mercutio, Benvolio,** *with five or six other* **Masquers** *and* **Torchbearers**

Romeo   What, shall this speech be spoke for our excuse?
Or shall we on without apology?

Benvolio   The date is out of such prolixity.
We'll have no Cupid hoodwinked with a scarf,
5   Bearing a Tartar's painted bow of lath,
Scaring the ladies like a crowkeeper,
Nor no without-book prologue, faintly spoke
After the prompter, for our entrance.
But let them measure us by what they will,
10   We'll measure them a measure and be gone.

Romeo   Give me a torch, I am not for this ambling.
Being but heavy I will bear the light.

Mercutio   Nay, gentle Romeo, we must have you dance.

Romeo   Not I, believe me. You have dancing shoes
15   With nimble soles, I have a soul of lead
So stakes me to the ground I cannot move.

Mercutio   You are a lover, borrow Cupid's wings
And soar with them above a common bound.

Romeo   I am too sore enpierced with his shaft
20   To soar with this light feathers, and so bound
I cannot bound a pitch above dull woe.
Under love's heavy burden do I sink.

A street. **Romeo, Mercutio,** *and* **Benvolio** *enter with five or six other* **Maskers** *and* **Torchbearers.**

Romeo   Well, shall we give the usual formal speech, or just go on in without an excuse?

Benvolio   This is too out of date. In our masking routine, let's have no blindfolded Cupid carrying a painted wooden bow and scaring the ladies like a scarecrow. And let's not make our entrance with memorized speeches, spoken in a weak voice with the help of a prompter. Let them judge us however they want. We'll have a dance and then leave.

Romeo   Let me carry a torch. I'm not one for this posing and posturing dance. Since I'm so heavy-hearted, I'll carry the light.

Mercutio   No, gentle Romeo, you must dance!

Romeo   Not I, believe me. You have dancing shoes with light-stepping soles. I have a soul of lead that holds me to the ground so I can't move.

Mercutio   But you're in love! Borrow Cupid's wings and soar high above the ground!

Romeo   I'm too sore from being wounded by his arrow to soar on such light feathers as his. I'm so weighted down that I can't leap higher than my sorrow. I'm sinking under the heavy burden of love.

Mercutio And, to sink in it, should you burden love –
Too great oppression for a tender thing.

25 **Romeo** Is love a tender thing? It is too rough,
Too rude, too boisterous, and it pricks like a thorn.

Mercutio If love be rough with you, be rough with love;
Prick love for pricking and you beat love down.
Give me a case to put my visage in:
30 A visor for a visor. What care I
What curious eye doth quote deformities?
Here are the beetle brows shall blush for me.

Benvolio Come, knock and enter, and no sooner in
But every man betake him to his legs.

35 **Romeo** A torch for me. Let wantons light of heart
Tickle the senseless rushes with their heels,
For I am proverbed with a grandsire phrase –
I'll be a candle-holder and look on.
The game was ne'er so fair, and I am dun.

40 **Mercutio** Tut, dun's the mouse, the constable's own word.
If thou art Dun we'll draw thee from the mire
Of – save your reverence – love, wherein thou stickest
Up to the ears. Come, we burn daylight, ho.

Romeo Nay, that's not so.

45 **Mercutio**   I mean sir, in delay
We waste our lights in vain, light lights by day.
Take our good meaning, for our judgement sits
Five times in that ere once in our five wits.

Romeo And we mean well in going to this masque,
50 But 'tis no wit to go.

Mercutio   Why, may one ask?

Romeo I dreamt a dream tonight.

Mercutio   And so did I.

Mercutio But when you sink in love, you become a burden to love—too great a burden for such a tender thing to carry.

Romeo Is love a tender thing? It's too rough, too rude, too quarrelsome. It pricks like a thorn.

Mercutio If love is rough with you, then you be rough with love! Prick love back for pricking you, and you'll beat love down. Give me a mask to cover my face: a mask for my ugly face. What do I care if curious eyes stare at the deformities? Here are the beetle brows of a mask that will blush for me!

Benvolio Okay, knock on the door and let's go in. As soon as we're inside, every man should start dancing.

Romeo As for me, I'll carry the torch. Let you lighthearted people tickle the carpet with your heels. I'll follow an old proverb about safety: I'll be the candle-holder and just watch. The party's at its brightest and most colorful now, but I feel like the color dun—drab and gray.

Mercutio Look, dun's the color of a mouse, so keep quiet as a mouse, as the constable said. But if you're the horse named Dun, we'll pull you out of the mud, or rather—pardon me—out of the mud of love, where you're stuck up to your ears. Let's go, we're wasting daylight.

Romeo Now that's not so—it's dark!

Mercutio I mean, sir, that by delaying we waste our torchlights, like lighting lights during the day. Take the obvious meaning. There's five times more wisdom in that than in one clever interpretation of the meaning.

Romeo And we mean well in going to this party, but it isn't wise to go.

Mercutio Why, may I ask?

Romeo I dreamed a dream last night.

Mercutio And so did I.

Romeo Well, what was yours?

55 **Mercutio**   That dreamers often lie.

Romeo In bed asleep, while they do dream things true.

Mercutio O then I see Queen Mab hath been with you.
She is the fairies' midwife, and she comes
In shape no bigger than an agate stone
60 On the forefinger of an alderman,
Drawn with a team of little atomies
Over men's noses as they lie asleep.
Her chariot is an empty hazelnut
Made by the joiner squirrel or old grub,
65 Time out o' mind the fairies' coachmakers;
Her waggon-spokes made of long spinners' legs,
The cover of the wings of grasshoppers,
Her traces of the smallest spider web,
Her collars of the moonshine's watery beams,
70 Her whip of cricket's bone, the lash of film,
Her waggoner a small grey-coated gnat,
Not half so big as a round little worm
Pricked from the lazy finger of a maid;
And in this state she gallops night by night
75 Through lovers' brains, and then they dream of love;
O'er courtiers' knees, that dream on curtsies straight;
O'er lawyers' fingers who straight dream on fees;
O'er ladies' lips, who straight on kisses dream,
Which oft the angry Mab with blisters plagues
80 Because their breaths with sweetmeats tainted are.
Sometimes she gallops o'er a courtier's nose
And then dreams he of smelling out a suit;
And sometime comes she with a tithe-pig's tail,
Tickling a parson's nose as a lies asleep;
85 Then dreams he of another benefice.
Sometime she driveth o'er a soldier's neck
And then dreams he of cutting foreign throats,
Of breaches, ambuscados, Spanish blades,

Romeo   Well, what was yours?

Mercutio   That dreamers often lie—

Romeo   —in bed asleep, while they dream things that are true.

Mercutio   Oh, then I see Queen Mab has been with you. She's the fairy who brings men's fantasies to life. She comes in a shape no bigger than a gemstone on the finger of an alderman. A team of tiny creatures draws her chariot over men's noses as they lie asleep. Her chariot is an empty hazelnut made by a squirrel cabinetmaker or an old worm, who have been the fairies' coachmakers since times too old to remember. The spokes of her wagon wheels are made of long spider's legs; the canopy is made of the wings of grasshoppers; her harnesses are of the smallest spider web; her collars are of moonbeams; her whip of cricket's bone; the lash of gossamer. Her driver is a small gray-coated gnat, not half as big as a round little worm that's pricked off the finger of a lazy maiden. In this way she gallops night after night through lovers' brains, and then they dream of love. Over courtiers' knees, who at once dream of making graceful curtsies; over lawyers' fingers who just then dream of fees. Over ladies' lips (which the angry Mab often plagues with blisters, because their breaths are tainted with sweet foods), who at once dream of kisses. Sometimes she gallops over a courtier's nose, who then dreams of smelling out a paid commission to influence the king. And sometimes, while she carries the tail of a pig who was paid to the church as an offering, she tickles a parson's nose with it as he lies asleep. And then he dreams of getting an additional parish. Sometimes she drives over a soldier's neck. Then he dreams of cutting enemies' throats, of breaking through enemy defenses, of ambushes, Spanish swords, long drinking bouts.

Of healths five fathom deep; and then anon
90   Drums in his ear, at which he starts and wakes,
And being thus frighted swears a prayer or two
And sleeps again. This is that very Mab
That plaits the manes of horses in the night
And bakes the elf-locks in foul sluttish hairs,
95   Which, once untangled, much misfortune bodes.
This the hag, when maids lie on their backs,
That presses them and learns them first to bear,
Making them women of good carriage.
This is she –

100 **Romeo**   Peace, peace, Mercutio, peace.
Thou talk'st of nothing.

Mercutio   True, I talk of dreams,
Which are the children of an idle brain,
Begot of nothing but vain fantasy,
105 Which is as thin of substance as the air
And more inconstant than the wind, who woos
Even now the frozen bosom of the north
And, being angered, puffs away from thence
Turning his face to the dew-dropping south.

110 **Benvolio** This wind you talk of blows us from ourselves:
Supper is done and we shall come too late.

Romeo I fear too early for my mind misgives
Some consequence yet hanging in the stars
Shall bitterly begin his fearful date
115 With this night's revels, and expire the term
Of a despised life closed in my breast
By some vile forfeit of untimely death.
But he that hath the steerage of my course
Direct my suit. On, lusty gentlemen.

120 **Benvolio** Strike, drum.

[*Exeunt*]

And then she drums in his ear, and he wakes up startled, and being frightened, he swears a prayer or two and goes back to sleep. This is the same Mab who knots the manes of horses during the night, and mats the hair of foul old hags. And when the hair is untangled, it is a sign of misfortune to come. This is the hag who, when maids lie on their backs, presses on them and teaches them to bear children, making them "women of good carriage." This is she—

Romeo   Stop, stop, Mercutio! Be quiet! You're talking nonsense.

Mercutio   True, I talk of dreams, which are the children of an idle brain. They are made of nothing but foolish fantasy, which is as thin as the air, more changeable than the wind, which first blows toward the frozen north—and then, becoming angry, turns away and blows toward the rainy south.

Benvolio   This wind you talk of blows us away from our plans. Supper's over, and we're going to arrive too late.

Romeo   Too early, I'm afraid. I have a strange feeling that something, influenced by the stars, is about to happen. It will begin its bitter course with tonight's festivities. It will end my hateful life by the evil of an early death. But God, who guides my life, will direct my path. Let's go, gentlemen.

Benvolio   Strike the drum!

[*They exit*]

Act I

Scene V

Capulet's house. Enter the **Masquers. Servants** *come forth with napkins*

First Servant Where's Potpan that he helps not to take away? He shift a trencher! He scrape a trencher!

Second Servant When good manners shall lie all in one or two men's hands, and they unwashed too, 'tis a foul thing.

5 **First Servant** Away with the joint-stools, remove the court-cupboard, look to the plate. Good thou, save me a piece of marchpane, and as thou loves me, let the porter let in Susan Grindstone and Nell [*Exit* **Second Servant**] [*Enter* **Antony** *and* **Potpan**] – Antony, and Potpan!

10 **Antony** Ay boy, ready.

First Servant You are looked for and called for, asked for and sought for, in the great chamber.

Potpan We cannot be here and there too. Cheerly, boys! Be brisk awhile, and the longer liver take all.

[*Exeunt* **Servants**]

Capulet's house. **Romeo** *and the* **Maskers** *enter and move to the side, looking on. Two* **Servants** *enter.*

First Servant Where's Potpan, who should be helping to clear the tables? What, him? Pick up a dish? Him? Scrape a plate?

Second Servant It's a terrible thing when good work habits fall to one or two men's hands, and those unwashed, too!

First Servant Put away the stools. Remove the sideboard. Take care of the silverplate. Good fellow, save me a piece of the dessert, marzipan. And do something for me: Tell the porter to let in Susan Grindstone and Nell.

[*The* **Second Servant** *exits*]

[**Antony** *and* **Potpan** *enter*]

Antony! Potpan!

Antony Here, fellow! I'm ready!

First Servant People are looking and calling for you in the great hall!

Potpan We can't be here and there too. Cheer up, fellows! Be happy while you can, and whoever lives the longest take it all!

[*The* **Servants** *exit*]

[*Enter* **Capulet, Lady Capulet, Juliet, Tybalt, Nurse** *and all the* **Guests** *and* **Gentlewomen** *to the* **Masquers**]

15 **Capulet** Welcome, gentlemen, ladies that have their toes
Unplagued with corns will have a bout with you.
Ah ha, my mistresses! Which of you all
Will now deny to dance? She that makes dainty,
She I'll swear hath corns. Am I come near ye now?
20 Welcome gentlemen. I have seen the day
That I have worn a visor and could tell
A whispering tale in a fair lady's ear,
Such as would please. 'Tis gone, 'tis gone, 'tis gone,
You are welcome, gentlemen: come, musicians, play.
25 A hall, a hall, give room! And foot it girls!

[*Music plays and they dance*]

More light, you knaves, and turn the tables up.
And quench the fire, the room is grown too hot.
Ah sirrah, this unlooked-for sport comes well.
Nay sit, nay sit, good cousin Capulet,
30 For you and I are past our dancing days.
How long is't now since last yourself and I
Were in a masque?

Cousin Capulet By'r Lady, thirty years.

Capulet What, man, 'tis not so much, 'tis not so much.
35 'Tis since the nuptial of Lucentio,
Come Pentecost as quickly as it will,
Some five and twenty years: and then we masqued.

Cousin Capulet 'Tis more, 'tis more, his son is elder, sir:
His son is thirty.

40 **Capulet** Will you tell me that?
His son was but a ward two years ago.

[**Capulet, Lady Capulet, Juliet, Tybalt,** *and the* **Nurse** *enter with the* **Guests** *and* **Maskers**]

Capulet Welcome, gentlemen! Ladies who don't have corns on their toes will have a dance with you. Aha, my ladies! Which of you will now refuse to dance? If one of you acts coy, I'll swear she has corns! Have I persuaded you? Welcome, gentlemen. I've seen the day when I have worn a mask and could whisper sweet words in a beautiful girl's ear that would delight her. But that time is gone, it's gone, it's gone. You are welcome, gentlemen. Come, musicians, play! We need the hall. Clear the room! Now go on, girls.

[*Music plays and dancing begins*]

More light, you dunces! Fold up the tables. Put out the fire; the room is getting too hot. Aha, these unexpected maskers come at a good time! [*To his* **Cousin**] Sit down, sit down, good cousin Capulet. You and I are past our dancing days. How long has it been now since you and I last wore masks?

Cousin Capulet By Our Lady—thirty years!

Capulet What, man? It hasn't been that long! Not that long! It was at the wedding of Lucentio, come Pentecost Sunday, about twenty-five years ago. We masked then!

Cousin Capulet It's more. It's more. His son is older than that, sir. His son is thirty.

Capulet Don't tell me that! His son was just a child two years ago!

Romeo What lady's that which doth enrich the hand
  Of yonder knight?

Servant   I know not, sir.

45 **Romeo** O, she doth teach the torches to burn bright.
  It seems she hangs upon the cheek of night
  As a rich jewel in an Ethiop's ear –
  Beauty too rich for use, for earth too dear.
  So shows a snowy dove trooping with crows
50 As yonder lady o'er her fellows shows.
  The measure done, I'll watch her place of stand,
  And touching hers, make blessed my rude hand.
  Did my heart love till now? Forswear it, sight.
  For I ne'er saw true beauty till this night.

55 **Tybalt** This by his voice should be a Montague.
  Fetch me my rapier, boy. What, dares the slave
  Come hither, covered with an antic face
  To fleer and scorn at our solemnity?
  Now by the stock and honour of my kin,
60 To strike him dead I hold it not a sin.

Capulet Why how now, kinsman, wherefore storm you so?

Tybalt Uncle, this is a Montague, our foe:
  A villain that is hither come in spite
  To scorn at our solemnity this night.

65 **Capulet** Young Romeo is it?

Tybalt   'Tis he, that villain Romeo.

Capulet Content thee, gentle coz, let him alone,
  'A bears him like a portly gentleman;
  And, to say truth, Verona brags of him
70 To be a virtuous and well-governed youth.
  I would not for the wealth of all this town
  Here in my house do him disparagement.
  Therefore, be patient, take no note of him.

Romeo [*spotting* **Juliet**] Who is the lady who is such an ornament on the hand of that gentleman?

Servant I don't know, sir.

Romeo Oh, she shows the torches how to burn bright! She seems to be a brilliant ornament of the night, like a rich jewel in an Ethiopian's ear. Her beauty is too rich for everyday use, too valuable for this earth. As a snow-white dove stands out among a troop of crows, so does that lady stand out among the crowd. When the dance is done, I'll watch where she goes, and I'll make my rough hand blessed by touching hers. Did my heart love before tonight? Then deny it, my eyes. For I've never seen true beauty until this night.

Tybalt By the sound of his voice, I think this is a Montague. Get me my sword, boy. How dare that lowlife come here, wearing a hideous mask to mock and make fun of our festivities? Now by my ancestors and my family's honor, I wouldn't call it a sin to strike him dead!

Capulet Well hello, kinsman! What's making you so angry?

Tybalt Uncle, this is a Montague, our enemy. He's a villain who's come here to be spiteful and to mock our occasion tonight!

Capulet Young Romeo, is it?

Tybalt That's him, that villain Romeo.

Capulet Calm down, gentle cousin. Let him alone. He's behaving himself like a real gentleman. And to tell the truth, Verona brags about him as a virtuous and well-behaved youth. I would not be impolite to him in my house for all the wealth of this town. So be patient, and ignore him.

It is my will, the which if thou respect,
75 Show a fair presence and put off these frowns,
An ill-beseeming semblance for a feast.

Tybalt It fits when such a villain is a guest:
I'll not endure him.

Capulet   He shall be endured.
80 What, goodman boy! I say he shall! Go to,
Am I the master here or you? Go to.
You'll not endure him! God shall mend my soul,
You'll make a mutiny among my guests,
You will set cock-a-hoop, you'll be the man!

85 **Tybalt** Why, uncle, 'tis a shame.

Capulet   Go to, go to.
You are a saucy boy. Is't so indeed?
This trick may chance to scathe you, I know what.
You must contrary me. Marry, 'tis time –
90 Well said, my hearts – You are a princox, go
Be quiet, or – More light! More light! – For shame,
I'll make you quiet. What, cheerly, my hearts!

Tybalt Patience perforce with wilful choler meeting
Makes my flesh tremble in their different greeting.
95 I will withdraw; but this intrusion shall
Now seeming sweet, convert to bitterest gall.

[*Exit*]

Romeo If I profane with my unworthiest hand
This holy shrine, the gentle sin is this:
My lips, two blushing pilgrims, ready stand
100 To smooth that rough touch with a tender kiss.

Juliet Good pilgrim, you do wrong your hand too much,
Which mannerly devotion shows in this;
For saints have hands that pilgrims' hands do touch,
And palm to palm is holy palmers' kiss.

It's my wish. If you respect it, you'll wear a pleasant face and stop this scowling, which isn't a suitable expression for a feast.

Tybalt It's a suitable expression when such a villain is a guest. I won't endure him being here!

Capulet He *shall* be endured! Who do you think you are, boy? I say he shall! [*Getting angry*] Well! Am I the master here or are you? Well now! You won't endure him! God save my soul, you'll cause a riot among my guests. You'll prance around boasting! You'll be the man!

Tybalt Why, uncle, it's shameful!

Capulet Well now, well! You're a smart-aleck boy. Is it shameful, indeed? This behavior may get you in trouble, I can tell you. You're going to cross me? Well, it's time— [*To his dancing guests*] Well done, my dears— [*To* **Tybalt**] You're a conceited, cocky young man! Go, or be quiet, or— [*To the* **Servants**] More light! More light!— [*To* **Tybalt**] For shame, I'll make sure you're quiet. [*To his guests*] Wonderful, my dears!

Tybalt [*to himself*] Being forced to be patient when he's so willfully angry makes me shake with anger. I'll go. This intrusion by Montague may seem all right now, but it will change to the bitterest feelings later.

[**Tybalt** *exits*]

Romeo [*taking* **Juliet's** *hand*] If I defile this holy shrine with my unworthy hand, then the gentler sin will be this: My lips, like two blushing pilgrims, stand ready to smooth that rough touch with a tender kiss.

Juliet Good pilgrim, you do your hand too much wrong. Your hand is showing pious devotion. The statues of saints have hands that pilgrims touch with their own hands. Placing a palm on the saint's palm is the holy pilgrim's kiss.

105 **Romeo** Have not saints lips, and holy palmers too?

Juliet Ay, pilgrim, lips that they must use in prayer.

Romeo O then, dear saint, let lips do what hands do!
They pray. Grant thou, lest faith turn to despair.

Juliet Saints do not move, though grant for prayer's sake.

110 **Romeo** Then move not, while my prayer's effect I take.
Thus from my lips, by thine, my sin is purged.

Juliet Then have my lips the sin that they have took.

Romeo Sin from my lips? O trespass sweetly urged!
Give me my sin again.

115 **Juliet**   You kiss by the book.

Nurse Madam, your mother craves a word with you.

Romeo What is her mother?

Nurse   Marry, bachelor,
Her mother is the lady of the house,
120 And a good lady, and a wise and virtuous.
I nursed her daughter that you talked withal.
I tell you, he that can lay hold of her
Shall have the chinks.

Romeo   Is she a Capulet?
125 O dear account! My life is my foe's debt.

Benvolio Away, be gone; the sport is at the best.

Romeo Ay, so I fear; the more is my unrest.

Capulet Nay, gentlemen, prepare not to be gone,
We have a trifling foolish banquet towards.
130 Is it e'en so? Why then, I thank you all;
I thank you honest gentlemen, good night.
More torches here. Come on then, let's to bed.

Romeo Don't saints have lips, and don't holy pilgrims have them too?

Juliet Yes, pilgrim. Lips that they must use in prayer.

Romeo Well then, dear saint, let lips do what hands do! They pray: "Grant me a kiss, or my faith may turn to despair."

Juliet Saints don't move, but they do grant prayers.

Romeo Then don't move, while I receive the benefit of my prayer. [**Romeo** *kisses* **Juliet**] So, the sin from my lips is washed away by your lips.

Juliet Then my lips have the sin that they've taken from yours.

Romeo Sin from my lips? How sweetly you tell me that I have sinned against you! Give me my sin back again. [*He kisses her again*]

Juliet You kiss in a very proper way!

Nurse Madam, your mother wishes a word with you.

Romeo Who is her mother?

Nurse Well, young sir, her mother is the lady of the house. And she's a good lady, wise and virtuous. I nursed her daughter, to whom you were talking. I tell you, the man that can win her shall have some money.

Romeo Is she a Capulet? A terrible accounting! Now my life is in debt to my enemy.

Benvolio Come on, let's go. The best of the party is over.

Romeo Yes, I'm afraid so—which makes me more uneasy.

Capulet No, gentlemen, don't leave yet. We'll soon be serving some light refreshments. Is that so? Well, then, I thank you all. Thank you, good gentlemen. Good night. Bring more

Ah, sirrah, by my fay, it waxes late.
I'll to my rest.

[*Exeunt all but* **Juliet** *and* **Nurse**]

135   **Juliet**   Come hither Nurse. What is yond gentleman?

Nurse   The son and heir of old Tiberio.

Juliet   What's he that now is going out of door?

Nurse   Marry, that I think be young Petruchio.

Juliet   What's he that follows here, that would not dance?

140   **Nurse**   I know not.

Juliet   Go ask his name. If he be married,
My grave is like to be my wedding bed.

Nurse   His name is Romeo, and a Montague,
The only son of your great enemy.

145   **Juliet**   My only love sprung from my only hate.
Too early seen unknown, and known too late.
Prodigious birth of love it is to me
That I must love a loathed enemy.

Nurse   What's this? What's this?

150   **Juliet**   A rhyme I learned even now
Of one I danced withal.

[*One calls within 'Juliet!'*]

Nurse   Anon, anon!
Come, let's away. The strangers are all gone.

[*Exeunt*]

torches here. Come on then, let's go to bed. Well, servant, on my faith, it's getting late. I'm off to my rest.

[*Everyone exits but* **Juliet** *and the* **Nurse**]

Juliet Come here, Nurse. Who is that gentleman there?

Nurse The son and heir of old Tiberio.

Juliet Who's the one that's going out the door now?

Nurse My, I think that's young Petruchio.

Juliet Who's the one that follows behind the others, the one who wouldn't dance?

Nurse I don't know.

Juliet Go ask his name. If he's married, then my wedding bed will be my grave.

Nurse [*returning after asking*] His name is Romeo, and he's a Montague. He's the only son of your great enemy.

Juliet The only one I love is the son of the only one I hate. When I first saw him, I didn't know who he was. Now, too late, I know! What an ominous first love for me—that I must love a hated enemy!

Nurse What's this? What's this?

Juliet A rhyme I just learned from someone I danced with.

[**Juliet's** *mother calls her*]

Nurse In a minute! In a minute! Come on, let's go. The guests have all gone.

[**Juliet** *and the* **Nurse** *exit*]

Comprehension   **Check What You Know**

1. What is the source of the tension in the first scene? Why are the characters upset?

2. What plans do Capulet and Lady Capulet have for Juliet?

3. What does Romeo learn when he speaks with the Clown?

4. How does Romeo describe the woman he loves in Scene 1?

5. Describe the Nurse's relationship with Juliet. How long has she known Juliet?

6. Romeo and his friends also have a plan in Act 1. What do they do and why do they do it?

7. Describe Romeo's reaction when he first sees Juliet.

8. Explain how Romeo changes within Act 1. What troubles him at the beginning of this act? What changes for him at the end of the act?

9. Compare Scene 1 and Scene 3. How do the characters display their emotions?

Activities & Role-Playing   **Classes or Book Clubs**

Ready for Anything Take the roles of Sampson, Gregory, Abraham, Benvolio, and Tybalt. Role-play Scene 1 before the officers enter the scene. Imagine that you feel threatened, tense, and edgy. Portray the way the characters might be holding their swords. Are they all brave or experienced swordsmen? What kind of "stake" do they have in the fight? How would they walk up to the enemy group?

A Room of Their Own Design the set or room for Scene 3 as Lady Capulet, Juliet, and the Nurse speak together. Include furniture and other items that might make them comfortable for this type of conversation. Make a model of your set design or create a drawing. Where and how do you think the characters might stand or sit as they talk?

Discussion Classes or Book Clubs

1. Refer to Mercutio's lines in Act 1. What kind of friend is he for Romeo? Would you like to have him for a friend?

2. Discuss the Prologue and what you already know about the play. If you were Romeo and Juliet, would you follow love or stay loyal to your family and friends? Explain your reasons.

3. Study the Nurse's character and discuss her role within the Capulet family.

Suggestions for Writing Improve Your Skills

1. Refer to the sonnet spoken by the Chorus in the Prologue to *Romeo and Juliet*. Study it for clues about writing a sonnet. A sonnet is a fourteen-line poem with a specific pattern. (It rhymes in a certain way and has a certain number and pattern of accented syllables per line.) Write a fourteen-line poem that expresses an emotion or details an opinion about an issue that is important to you. (Following all the "rules" for writing a traditional sonnet can be hard. If you're feeling adventurous, try to follow just one or two. For example, you might choose to end each line with a rhyme or include the same number of syllables in each line.)

2. Imagine you are a reporter observing the events in Scene 1. Write a newspaper article summarizing what's going on in Verona. You might want to remember that reporters try to let readers know the five "W"s: who, what, where, when, and why! Refer to the Prologue for facts about the history of the two families that might be helpful information for your readers. Include a few sentences from the Prince, as if you had an interview with him.

All the World's a Stage Introduction

Head over heels in anger or in love—that describes the mood for the young characters in the play. And their love is either very strong or disappears in an instant. Romeo is such a young person. He has barely noticed the increased fighting between his family and their enemies, the Capulets. Then he hears about a party by chance. To get into the party, he pretends to be a masker and crashes the event. Once he gets there he forgets all about one love interest and finds a new one. But this time, the two that fall in love are enemies.

What's in a Name? Characters

What's in a name? Maybe a great deal. Romeo's name suits his *rom*antic character. Mercutio makes fun of Tybalt's name, the name of a cat in a popular story. Mercutio lives up to his name because of his *mercu*rial—changing—temperament. He is hot-tempered, quick-witted, and moody.

Often, Romeo and Juliet depict their feelings in terms of falconry—an ancient form of hunting still popular in Shakespeare's day. Falcons needed to be wild enough to hunt prey such as small birds and tame enough to return. Romeo and Juliet playfully use these ideas of feeling free or feeling bound when they describe their love.

COME WHAT MAY Things to Watch For

Can it last? For Romeo and Juliet and for most other couples, falling in love means creating a private, intense, separate world of romantic joy. Unfortunately, the outside world keeps crashing in.

Other characters offer advice when they can. Friar Lawrence, Mercutio, and the Nurse all try to act as friends. But they may not always understand what's at stake. When Romeo and Juliet follow their hearts, are they also using their heads? Who is offering good advice? Who is leading them down a wrong path?

All Our Yesterdays Historical and Social Context

People in hiding, in prison, or put to horrible deaths—this is often the result of no religious freedom. And this was what carried the day for a very long time—especially in England.

In England, the hate and violence shifted depending on who was the king or queen. Henry VIII (1509–1547), Edward VI (1547–1553), and Mary I (1553–1558) ruled with very violent acts against people based on religion.

Mary, who was Catholic, executed so many Protestants she was known as "Bloody Mary."

In 1558, Elizabeth I became queen. Elizabeth, who was Protestant, was very popular. Under her, people did not fear being treated with such violence because of their religion. However, most Catholics kept their faith to themselves. They were expected to attend Protestant services and were fined if they didn't. Attending mass could land you in jail. In a way, the events of the play in Italy would have been somewhat foreign to the audience. Seeing a Catholic friar for help just didn't fit into the Elizabethan world. Some audience members might have been skeptical about taking this Catholic priest's advice.

The Play's the Thing Staging

"O Romeo, Romeo, wherefore art thou Romeo?" Many people who have never seen *Romeo and Juliet* can still recognize this famous line. It occurs in Act 2, Scene 2, as Juliet stands alone at her balcony and calls out into the night.

The play's first audiences would have had to imagine part of this setting. Staged in an outdoor theater, this night scene would have actually taken place in the afternoon. Juliet was played by a boy in female costume. And she might not have been alone on the balcony. The balcony was set in the stage's back wall. There the richest and most powerful audience members watched the play. Like modern-day skyboxes, these seats offered excellent views and served as a status symbol. As he cried out Romeo's name, the actor playing Juliet may have been surrounded by the people in those very high seats.

My Words Fly Up Language

Mercutio is full of clever jokes. Some of these are quite brainy. Some are meant to entertain the "lowbrows" in the audience. In Act 2, Scene 4, when Mercutio calls the Nurse a "bawd," he's saying that she's still a lustful woman. *Bawd* could also be applied to someone who arranged sexual encounters for others. In addition, *bawd* meant "rabbit" or "hare." But that's not the end of the joke—*hare* could be a slang word for "prostitute." So could "goose."

Mercutio also pokes fun at Romeo by comparing his ladylove to famous women of legend. The most important is Laura, loved by the 14th-century Italian poet Petrarch. Romeo often expresses his feelings in ways that echo Petrarch's poems to Laura.

In Scene 4, Mercutio accuses Romeo of being "counterfeit" because he avoided his friends and gave them "the slip." In Shakespeare's England, "the slip" also meant counterfeit cash.

Act II

Prologue

Enter **Chorus**

Chorus Now old desire doth in his deathbed lie
And young affection gapes to be his heir;
That fair for which love groaned for and would die,
With tender Juliet matched, is now not fair.
5 Now Romeo is beloved, and loves again,
Alike bewitched by the charm of looks;
But to his foe supposed he must complain,
And she steal love's sweet bait from fearful hooks.
Being held a foe, he may not have access
10 To breathe such vows as lovers use to swear;
And she as much in love, her means much less
To meet her new beloved any where.
But passion lends them power, time means, to meet,
Tempering extremities with extreme sweet.

[*Exit*]

*The **Chorus** enters.*

Chorus   The old infatuation is now dead, and a new love longs to replace it. The beautiful woman, previously longed for and worth dying for, doesn't seem as beautiful when compared to tender Juliet. Now Romeo is in love again, and he is loved in return. He and Juliet are mutually enchanted by the charm of gazing at one another. But he must woo an alleged foe, and she must steal love's sweet bait from a dangerous trap. Since he's considered an enemy, he isn't free to see her and make the usual promises of love. And though she is just as much in love, she has even fewer means to meet her new sweetheart anywhere. Nevertheless, their passion motivates them. Time grants them opportunities to meet, and their troubles are moderated by these sweet meetings.

[*The **Chorus** exits*]

Act II

Scene I

A lane by the wall of Capulet's orchard. Enter **Romeo**

Romeo Can I go forward when my heart is here?
Turn back, dull earth, and find thy centre out.

[*Enter* **Benvolio** *and* **Mercutio**]

Benvolio Romeo! My cousin, Romeo! Romeo!

Mercutio   He is wise,
5   And, on my life, hath stolen him home to bed.

Benvolio He ran this way, and leapt this orchard wall.
Call, good Mercutio.

Mercutio   Nay, I'll conjure too.
Romeo! Humours! Madman! Passion! Lover!
10   Appear thou in the likeness of a sigh,
Speak but one rhyme and I am satisfied.
Cry but 'Ay, me!' Pronounce but 'love' and 'dove',
Speak to my gossip Venus one fair word,
One nickname for her purblind son and heir,
15   Young Abraham Cupid, he that shot so trim
When King Cophetua loved the beggar maid.
He heareth not, he stirreth not, he moveth not;
The ape is dead, and I must conjure him.
I conjure thee by Rosaline's bright eyes,

A street by the wall of Capulet's orchard. **Romeo** *enters.*

Romeo How can I walk on, when my heart is here? Turn around, weary body, and follow your heart.

[**Benvolio** *and* **Mercutio** *enter*]

Benvolio Romeo! Cousin Romeo! Romeo!

Mercutio He's smart. I bet he got himself home to bed.

Benvolio He ran this way and climbed over this garden wall. Call him, Mercutio.

Mercutio Sure. I'll conjure him up. Romeo! Moody One! Maniac! Incurable Romantic! Lover! Appear in the form of a sigh. I'll be satisfied if you recite even one line of poetry. Just exclaim, "Oh, my!" Rhyme "love" and "dove." Speak one sweet word to my old crony, Venus. One nickname for her completely blind son and heir—Cupid, that ancient child, the one whose straight arrow caused King Cophetua to fall in love with a beggar maiden. Romeo doesn't hear me; he's not stirring; he's not moving. The silly ape is dead, and I must raise him back to life again. I summon you by the power of

20 By her high forehead and her scarlet lip.
By her fine foot, straight leg, and quivering thigh,
And the demesnes that there adjacent lie,
That in thy likeness thou appear to us.

Benvolio And if he hear thee, thou wilt anger him.

25 **Mercutio** This cannot anger him. 'Twould anger him
To raise a spirit in his mistress' circle
Of some strange nature, letting it there stand
Till she had laid it and conjured it down;
That were some spite. My invocation
30 Is fair and honest: in his mistress' name
I conjure only but to raise up him.

Benvolio Come, he hath hid himself among these trees
To be consorted with the humorous night.
Blind is his love, and best befits the dark.

35 **Mercutio** If love be blind, love cannot hit the mark.
Now will he sit under a medlar tree
And wish his mistress were that kind of fruit
As maids call medlars when they laugh alone.
O Romeo, that she were, O that she were
40 An open-arse and thou a poperin pear!
Romeo, good night. I'll to my truckle-bed.
This field-bed is too cold for me to sleep.
Come, shall we go?

Benvolio   Go then, for 'tis vain
45 To seek him here that means not to be found.

[*Exeunt* **Benvolio** *and* **Mercutio**]

Rosaline's bright eyes, by her elegant forehead and her ruby lips. By her dainty foot, long leg, and quivering thigh—and all the areas in between. Appear to us in your flesh and bone.

Benvolio   If he can hear you, he'll be angry.

Mercutio   This won't anger him. He'd be angry if I summoned a spirit to rise in his lover's circle, and let it stand there until she laid her spell on it and made it lie down. Now, that would provoke him. My spell is fair and honest. It's only in his beloved's name to arouse him.

Benvolio   Let's go. He's hiding in the trees to commune with the brooding night. His love is blind. It belongs in the dark.

Mercutio   Love that's blind is lost. Now he'll sit under an apple tree and wish his lover was the type of fruit whose suggestive shape young women snicker about. Oh Romeo! If only she was that kind of apple and you were a long pear! Good night, Romeo. I'm off to my cot. It's too cold for me to be camping out. Come on. Shall we go?

Benvolio   Yes. Let's go. It's useless to look for him when he doesn't want to be found.

[**Benvolio** *and* **Mercutio** *exit*]

Act II

Scene II

Capulet's orchard. Enter **Romeo**

Romeo   He jests at scars that never felt a wound.

[*Enter* **Juliet** *above*]

But soft, what light through yonder window breaks?
It is the east and Juliet is the sun!
Arise fair sun and kill the envious moon
5   Who is already sick and pale with grief
That thou her maid art far more fair than she.
Be not her maid since she is envious,
Her vestal livery is but sick and green
And none but fools do wear it. Cast it off.
10   It is my lady, O it is my love!
O that she knew she were!
She speaks, yet she says nothing. What of that?
Her eye discourses, I will answer it.
I am too bold. 'Tis not to me she speaks.
15   Two of the fairest stars in all the heaven,
Having some business, do entreat her eyes
To twinkle in their spheres till they return.
What if her eyes were there, they in her head?
The brightness of her cheek would shame those stars
20   As daylight doth a lamp. Her eyes in heaven
Would through the airy region stream so bright

Capulet's orchard. **Romeo** *enters.*

Romeo He makes fun of wounds he's never experienced.

[**Juliet** *enters, above*]

But hush. What's that light cracking through the window? It's as if Juliet is the sun, shining from the east! Arise, radiant sun, and overshadow the jealous moon. She's sick and pale with grief because you, her chaste servant, are so much more beautiful. Don't serve her, since she envies you. Her virgin's garments are washed out and green, and only court jesters wear them. Shed them. It's the lady I love! If only she knew that I loved her! She speaks, but I can't hear her. What of it? Her eyes speak to me, and I will answer them.
I'm too presumptuous. It's not me she's talking to. Two of heaven's most dazzling stars have begged her eyes to shine in their orbits, while they go off on some business. And what if her eyes really were there and the stars shone in her face? The brightness of her cheeks would outshine those stars like daylight outshines a lamp. Her eyes would glow so brightly in

That birds would sing and think it were not night.
See how she leans her cheek upon her hand.
O that I were a glove upon that hand,
25   That I might touch that cheek!

Juliet   Ay me!

Romeo   She speaks.
O speak again bright angel, for thou art
As glorious to this night, being o'er my head,
30   As is a winged messenger of heaven
Unto the white-upturned wondering eyes
Of mortals that fall back to gaze on him
When he bestrides the lazy-pacing clouds
And sails upon the bosom of the air.

35 **Juliet** O Romeo, Romeo, wherefore art thou Romeo?
Deny thy father and refuse thy name.
And I'll no longer be a Capulet.

Romeo Shall I hear more, or shall I speak at this?

Juliet 'Tis but thy name that is my enemy;
40   Thou art thyself, though not a Montague.
What's Montague? It is nor hand nor foot
Nor arm nor face nor any other part
Belonging to a man. O be some other name.
What's in a name? That which we call a rose
45   By any other word would smell as sweet.
So Romeo would, were he not Romeo called,
Retain that dear perfection which he owes
Without that title. Romeo, doff thy name,
And for that name, which is no part of thee,
50   Take all myself.

Romeo   I take thee at thy word.
Call me but love, and I'll be new baptised:
Henceforth I never will be Romeo.

the sky that birds would sing, thinking it was daybreak. Look at how she leans her face on her hand. How I wish I could be a glove on her hand, so that I could touch her cheek!

Juliet [*sighing*] Ay me!

Romeo She speaks. Oh, speak again, bright angel. Standing above me, you glorify this night like an angel from heaven that visits a marveling human. He staggers and gazes up with awestruck eyes at this angel, who mounts a lingering cloud and sails through the depths of the heavens.

Juliet Oh Romeo, Romeo. Why must you be Romeo? Deny your father and refuse your name. Or swear to be my love, and I will no longer be a Capulet.

Romeo [*to himself*] Should I listen to more, or should I speak now?

Juliet It's only your name that is my enemy. You would still be yourself if you were not a Montague. What is Montague? It's not a hand, or foot, or arm, or face, or any other part of a person. Oh, change your name. What's in a name? If what we call a rose were renamed, it would still smell just as sweet. So if Romeo weren't called Romeo, he would still retain his precious perfection. He possesses it regardless of his name. Romeo, get rid of your name, which isn't part of you, and in exchange take all of me.

Romeo [*to* **Juliet**] I'll take you at your word. Just call me "love," and I'll be reborn. From now on, I'm no longer Romeo.

Juliet What man art thou that thus bescreened in night
55   So stumblest on my counsel?

Romeo   By a name
     I know not how to tell thee who I am:
     My name, dear saint, is hateful to myself
     Because it is an enemy to thee.
60   Had I it written, I would tear the word.

Juliet My ears have yet not drunk a hundred words
     Of thy tongue's uttering, yet I know the sound.
     Art thou not Romeo, and a Montague?

Romeo Neither, fair maid, if either thee dislike.

65 **Juliet** How cam'st thou hither, tell me, and wherefore?
     The orchard walls are high and hard to climb,
     And the place death, considering who thou art,
     If any of my kinsmen find thee here.

Romeo With love's light wings did I o'erperch these walls,
70   For stony limits cannot hold love out,
     And what love can do, that dares love attempt:
     Therefore thy kinsmen are no stop to me.

Juliet If they do see thee, they will murder thee.

Romeo Alack, there lies more peril in thine eye
75   Than twenty of their swords. Look thou but sweet
     And I am proof against their enmity.

Juliet I would not for the world they saw thee here.

Romeo I have night's cloak to hide me from their eyes,
     And but thou love me, let them find me here.
80   My life were better ended by their hate
     Than death prorogued, wanting of thy love.

Juliet By whose direction found'st thou out this place?

Juliet Who's there, concealed in the dark and eavesdropping on my secret thoughts?

Romeo I don't know how to tell you who I am. My name, dear saint, is repulsive to me because it's your enemy. If I had written it, I would tear it up.

Juliet My ears have not even taken in a hundred words from your mouth, but I recognize your voice. Aren't you Romeo, and a Montague?

Romeo I'm neither, lovely lady, if either displeases you.

Juliet Tell me, how did you get here, and why? The orchard walls are high and hard to climb. And because of who you are, this place could be fatal to you if any of my relatives find you here.

Romeo I flew over these walls with love's light wings. Barriers of stone can't hold back love. And love takes risks to accomplish what it can. Therefore, your relatives can't hinder me.

Juliet If they see you, they'll kill you.

Romeo Oh! Your eyes are more dangerous than twenty of their swords. Only look upon me favorably, and I am immune to their hostility.

Juliet I would not want them to see you here for anything in the world.

Romeo The night's veil hides me from their sight. And if you will only love me, let them find me here. I'd rather have my life ended by their hatred than postpone death and live without your love.

Juliet Who showed you how to find me?

Romeo By love, that first did prompt me to enquire.
He lent me counsel, and I lent him eyes.
85   I am no pilot, yet wert thou as far
As that vast shore washed with the farthest sea,
I should adventure for such merchandise.

Juliet Thou knowest the mask of night is on my face,
Else would a maiden blush bepaint my cheek
90   For that which thou hast heard me speak tonight.
Fain would I dwell on form; fain, fain deny
What I have spoke. But farewell compliment!
Dost thou love me? I know thou wilt say 'Ay',
And I will take thy word. Yet, if thou swearest,
95   Thou mayst prove false. At lovers' perjuries,
They say, Jove laughs. O gentle Romeo,
If thou dost love, pronounce it faithfully.
Or, if thou think'st I am too quickly won,
I'll frown and be perverse and say thee nay,
100   So thou wilt woo; but else, not for the world.
In truth, fair Montague, I am too fond,
And therefore thou mayst think my haviour light,
But trust me, gentleman, I'll prove more true
Than those that have more cunning to be strange.
105   I should have been more strange, I must confess,
But that thou overheard'st, ere I was ware,
My true love's passion. Therefore pardon me,
And not impute this yielding to light love,
Which the dark night hath so discovered.

110 **Romeo** Lady, by yonder blessed moon I vow,
That tips with silver all these fruit-tree tops –

Juliet O swear not by the moon, th' inconstant moon,
That monthly changes in her circled orb,
Lest that thy love prove likewise variable.

115 **Romeo** What shall I swear by?

Romeo Love did, which first inspired me to seek you. He offered me advice, and I offered him my vision. I'm not a navigator, but even if you were as far away as a vast shore of the most remote sea, I would venture out to search for a treasure like you.

Juliet You know that the night obscures my face. Otherwise, a girlish blush would tint my cheeks because of what you overheard me say tonight. I'd like to observe the proper formalities and gladly, gladly deny what I said. But farewell, etiquette! Do you love me? I know you'll answer "yes," and I'll take your word for it. Yet, if you swear, you might prove untrue. They say the god Jupiter laughs at lovers' false oaths. Oh, gentle Romeo, if you love me, profess it faithfully. Or if you think I give in too easily, I'll frown and be stubborn, and I'll reject you so you'll keep pursuing me—otherwise, I wouldn't do that for the world. To tell you the truth, dear Montague, I'm too affectionate, and therefore you might think I'm not serious. But believe me, sir, I'll prove more faithful than those who play hard to get. I'll admit that I should have been more aloof. But without my being aware of it, you overheard my true feelings. So forgive me, and don't misinterpret this surrender as a frivolous love that the dark night has brought to light.

Romeo Lady, I vow by the blessed moon up there, whose light tips the leaves on top of the fruit trees silver—

Juliet Oh, don't swear by the moon!—not by the erratic moon, that changes as she makes her monthly rounds—in case your love turns out to be just as changeable.

Romeo What should I swear by?

Juliet   Do not swear at all;
    Or, if thou wilt, swear by thy gracious self,
    Which is the god of my idolatry,
    And I'll believe thee.

120   **Romeo**   If my heart's dear love –

Juliet Well, do not swear. Although I joy in thee,
    I have no joy of this contract tonight:
    It is too rash, too unadvised, too sudden,
    Too like the lightning, which doth cease to be
125   Ere one can say 'It lightens'. Sweet, good night.
    This bud of love, by summer's ripening breath,
    May prove a beauteous flower when next we meet.
    Good night, and good night! As sweet repose and rest
    Come to thy heart as that within my breast!

130   **Romeo** O wilt thou leave me so unsatisfied?

Juliet What satisfaction canst thou have tonight?

Romeo The exchange of thy love's faithful vow for mine.

Juliet I gave thee mine before thou didst request it,
    And yet I would it were to give again.

135   **Romeo** Wouldst thou withdraw it? For what purpose, love?

Juliet But to be frank and give it thee again;
    And yet I wish but for the thing I have.
    My bounty is as boundless as the sea,
    My love as deep; the more I give to thee
140   The more I have, for both are infinite.
    I hear some noise within. Dear love, adieu.

[**Nurse** *calls within*]

Anon, good Nurse! Sweet Montague be true.
Stay but a little, I will come again.

[*Exit* **Juliet**]

Juliet Don't swear at all. Or, if you must swear, swear by your gracious self, which is the god I worship. Then I'll believe you.

Romeo If my beloved, dear sweetheart—

Juliet Well, don't swear. Although I rejoice in you, I take no joy in these vows tonight. It's too rash, too ill-advised, too sudden, too much like lightning—which ends before you can say, "It's gotten light." Sweetheart, good night. By the time we next meet, this budlike beginning of love may have blossomed into a beautiful flower, ripened by the summer air. Good night, good night! May such sweet rest and sleep come to your heart as lies within mine.

Romeo Oh, will you leave me so unsatisfied?

Juliet What satisfaction can you have tonight?

Romeo Your vow of true love, exchanged for mine.

Juliet I gave you mine before you asked for it. And yet I wish I had it to give away again.

Romeo You'd like to take it back? Why, my love?

Juliet Only to be free with it and give it to you again. But I'm wishing for what I already have. My gifts are as boundless as the sea. My love is just as deep. The more I give to you, the more I have, for both are infinite. I hear a noise inside. Dear love, goodbye.

[*The* **Nurse** *calls from inside*]

[*To* **Nurse**] Just a minute, good Nurse! [*To* **Romeo**] Sweet Montague, be true. Wait just a little; I'll be back.

[**Juliet** *exits*]

Romeo O blessed, blessed night. I am afeard,
145   Being in night, all this is but a dream,
    Too flattering sweet to be substantial.

[*Enter* **Juliet** *above*]

Juliet Three words, dear Romeo, and good night indeed.
    If that thy bent of love be honourable,
    Thy purpose marriage, send me word tomorrow
150   By one that I'll procure to come to thee,
    Where and what time thou wilt perform the rite,
    And all my fortunes at thy foot I'll lay,
    And follow thee my lord throughout the world.

Nurse [*within*] Madam!

155 **Juliet** I come, anon – But if thou meanest not well
    I do beseech thee –

Nurse [*within*]   Madam!

Juliet   By and by I come –
    To cease thy strife and leave me to my grief.
160   Tomorrow will I send.

Romeo   So thrive my soul –

Juliet A thousand times good night.

[*Exit* **Juliet**]

Romeo A thousand times the worse, to want thy light.
    Love goes toward love as schoolboys from their books,
165   But love from love, toward school with heavy looks.

[*Enter* **Juliet** *above*]

Juliet Hist! Romeo, hist! O for a falconer's voice
    To lure this tassel-gentle back again.

Romeo Oh, blessed, blessed night. Because it's the night, I'm afraid that this is all a dream. It's too full of sweet fantasies to be real.

[**Juliet** *enters, above*]

Juliet Three more words, dear Romeo, and then goodnight for real. If your romantic intentions are honorable and your purpose is to get married, send me a message tomorrow (by someone I'll arrange to meet you) telling me where and when you'll perform the ceremony. And then I'll lay my whole life at your feet, and follow you as my lord throughout the world.

Nurse [*inside*] Madam!

Juliet I'll be there in a second— [*To* **Romeo**] But if you're not being sincere, I beg you—

Nurse [*inside*] Madam!

Juliet I'm coming right now— [*To* **Romeo**] To stop courting me and leave me alone to grieve. Tomorrow I'll send my messenger.

Romeo Upon my soul—

Juliet A thousand times, goodnight.

[**Juliet** *exits*]

Romeo I'm a thousand times worse off, without your light. Lovers run to each other the way schoolboys run from their books. But lovers say goodbye slowly and reluctantly, like schoolboys heading to class.

[**Juliet** *enters, above*]

Juliet Psst! Romeo! Psst! Oh, if only I had a voice like a falconer, to lure this noble hawk back again. Controlled by a

Bondage is hoarse and may not speak aloud,
Else would I tear the cave where Echo lies
170 And make her airy tongue more hoarse than mine
With repetition of my 'Romeo'.

Romeo It is my soul that calls upon my name.
How silver-sweet sound lovers' tongues by night,
Like softest music to attending ears.

175 **Juliet** Romeo!

Romeo   My dear?

Juliet   What o'clock tomorrow
Shall I send to thee?

Romeo   By the hour of nine.

180 **Juliet** I will not fail. 'Tis twenty year till then.
I have forgot why I did call thee back.

Romeo Let me stand here till thou remember it.

Juliet I shall forget, to have thee still stand there,
Remembering how I love thy company.

185 **Romeo** And I'll still stay, to have thee still forget,
Forgetting any other home but this.

Juliet 'Tis almost morning. I would have thee gone;
And yet no farther than a wanton's bird,
That lets it hop a little from her hand,
190 Like a poor prisoner in his twisted gyves,
And with a silk thread plucks it back again,
So loving-jealous of his liberty.

Romeo I would I were thy bird.

Juliet   Sweet, so would I.
195 Yet I should kill thee with much cherishing.
Good night, good night! Parting is such sweet sorrow
That I shall say good night till it be morrow.

[Exit]

strict father, I'm forced to speak low and quietly. If I weren't, I'd pierce the cave where the nymph Echo lives with my calls for "Romeo!" She'd grow hoarse calling out the echoes of my cries.

Romeo It's my soul who's calling out my name. How silvery-sweet lovers' voices sound in the night. It's like the softest music to listening ears.

Juliet Romeo!

Romeo My dear?

Juliet What time should I send my messenger to you tomorrow?

Romeo By nine o'clock.

Juliet I won't fail to do it. It feels like twenty years until then. I forgot why I called you back.

Romeo I'll stand here until you remember.

Juliet I'll forget, just to have you keep standing there, remembering only how I love your company.

Romeo And I'll keep waiting, so that you keep forgetting, and I'll forget I have any other home but this one.

Juliet It's almost morning. I would like you to go—but no further than a spoiled girl's bird. She lets it hop a little away from her hand, like a poor prisoner in his twisted chains. Then she pulls it back again with a silk thread, for she's so lovingly possessive and jealous of its freedom.

Romeo I wish I were your bird.

Juliet Sweet, so do I. But I'd kill you by cherishing you so much. Goodnight, goodnight! Parting is so sweetly sad that I could go on saying goodnight until the morning.

[**Juliet** *exits*]

Romeo Sleep dwell upon thine eyes, peace in thy breast!
Would I were sleep and peace, so sweet to rest!
200   Hence will I to my ghostly sire's close cell,
His help to crave and my dear hap to tell.

[Exit]

Romeo May sleep visit your eyes, and peace live in your breast! If only I were sleep and peace, to rest in such sweet places! I'll go to my father confessor's chamber, to beg for his help and tell him about my good fortune.

[**Romeo** *exits*]

Act II

Scene III

Friar Lawrence's cell. Enter **Friar Lawrence** *with a basket*

Friar Lawrence The gray-eyed morn smiles on the frowning
    night,
    Check'ring the eastern clouds with streaks of light;
    And fleckel'd darkness like a drunkard reels
5   From forth day's path and Titan's fiery wheels.
    Now, ere the sun advance his burning eye
    The day to cheer and night's dank dew to dry,
    I must up-fill this osier cage of ours
    With baleful weeds and precious-juiced flowers.
10   The earth that's nature's mother is her tomb;
    What is her burying grave, that is her womb.
    And from her womb children of divers kind
    We sucking on her natural bosom find;
    Many for many virtues excellent,
15   None but for some, and yet all different.
    O, mickle is the powerful grace that lies
    In plants, herbs, stones, and their true qualities;
    For nought so vile that on the earth doth live
    But to the earth some special good doth give;
20   Nor aught so good but, strained from that fair use,
    Revolts from true birth, stumbling on abuse:
    Virtue itself turns vice, being misapplied,
    And vice sometime's by action dignified.
    Within the infant rind of this weak flower

Friar Lawrence's chamber. **Friar Lawrence** *enters, carrying a basket.*

Friar Lawrence The gray-eyed morning lightens the gloomy night and smiles away night's frowns. Streaks of light pattern the eastern clouds. Like a drunkard, dappled darkness reels out of the way of the day and fiery sun. Now, before the sun raises its burning eye to brighten the world and to dry the night's dew, I must fill up our basket with harmful weeds and flowers that have precious juices. Earth is nature's mother, as well as nature's tomb. It's the grave in which everything gets buried, but also a womb. Many diverse living things spring from this womb and take nourishment from the earth. Numerous plants have many beneficial qualities and all of them are useful for some purpose, yet they are all different. Oh, there is great beneficial power in plants, herbs, stones, and their essences! Nothing that lives on the earth is so vile that it doesn't have some individual goodness that it can yield. And nothing is so good that its proper use can't be perverted or abused. Virtue itself becomes vice when it's misguided, and vice can be like virtue when it has a good result. [*Examining a flower from his basket*] This frail flower's young rind contains both poison and medicinal power. Smell this part of it and your whole body feels better.

25   Poison hath residence, and medicine power,
    For this, being smelt, with that part cheers each part;
    Being tasted, slays all senses with the heart.
    Two such opposed kings encamp them still
    In man as well as herbs – grace and rude will;
30   And where the worser is predominant,
    Full soon the canker death eats up that plant.

[*Enter* **Romeo**]

Romeo   Good morrow father!

Friar Lawrence   Benedicite!
    What early tongue so sweet saluteth me?
35   Young son, it argues a distempered head
    So soon to bid good morrow to thy bed.
    Care keeps watch in every old man's eye,
    And where care lodges sleep will never lie;
    But where unbruised youth with unstuffed brain
40   Doth couch his limbs, there golden sleep doth reign.
    Therefore thy earliness doth me assure
    Thou art uproused with some distemperature;
    Or if not so, then here I hit it right –
    Our Romeo hath not been in bed tonight.

45 **Romeo**   That last is true; the sweeter rest was mine.

Friar Lawrence   God pardon sin! Wast thou with Rosaline?

Romeo   With Rosaline, my ghostly father? No.
    I have forgot that name, and that name's woe.

Friar Lawrence   That's my good son; but where hast thou
50   been then?

Romeo   I'll tell thee ere thou ask it me again.
    I have been feasting with mine enemy,
    Where, on a sudden, one hath wounded me

But if you taste it, it kills you, and then you won't smell or taste anymore. And humankind is like herbs. Both people and herbs contain both good and evil, camped within them like two enemy armies. When evil is predominant, death's worm eats up the plant.

[**Romeo** *enters*]

Romeo Good morning, Father!

Friar Lawrence A blessing on you. Whose early-risen voice so sweetly hails me? Young son, leaving your bed so early suggests a disturbed mind. Worry keeps watch in the eyes of old men, and sleep will never visit those old eyes where worry lives. But golden sleep rules where trouble-free young men rest their limbs with clear minds. Therefore, your earliness tells me you're awake because something's upsetting you. Or if that's wrong, then here I've got it right: Our Romeo didn't go to bed tonight.

Romeo That last is true. I've had a sweeter rest.

Friar Lawrence God pardon sin! Were you with Rosaline?

Romeo With Rosaline, holy Father? No. I've forgotten that name and the pain that went with it.

Friar Lawrence That's my good son. But then where *have* you been?

Romeo I'll tell you before you have to ask me again. I have been to a party at my enemy's. There, suddenly someone whom I wounded also wounded me. Both of us can be cured

That's by me wounded. Both our remedies
55   Within thy help and holy physic lies.
I bear no hatred, blessed man, for lo,
My intercession likewise steads my foe.

Friar Lawrence   Be plain, good son, and homely in thy drift.
Riddling confession finds but riddling shrift.

60   **Romeo**   Then plainly know my heart's dear love is set
On the fair daughter of rich Capulet.
As mine on hers, so hers is set on mine;
And all combined, save what thou must combine
By holy marriage. When, and where, and how,
65   We met, we wooed, and made exchange of vow,
I'll tell thee as we pass; but this I pray,
That thou consent to marry us today.

Friar Lawrence   Holy Saint Francis! What a change is here!
Is Rosaline, that thou didst love so dear,
70   So soon forsaken? Young men's love, then, lies
Not truly in their hearts, but in their eyes.
Jesu Maria, what a deal of brine
Hath washed thy sallow cheeks for Rosaline!
How much salt water thrown away in waste,
75   To season love, that of it doth not taste!
The sun not yet thy sighs from heaven clears,
Thy old groans yet ring in mine ancient ears;
Lo, here upon thy cheek the stain doth sit
Of an old tear that is not washed off yet.
80   If e'er thou wast thyself, and these woes thine,
Thou and these woes were all for Rosaline.
And art thou changed? Pronounce this sentence, then:
Women may fall, when there's no strength in men.

Romeo   Thou chid'st me oft for loving Rosaline.

85   **Friar Lawrence**   For doting, not for loving, pupil mine.

Romeo   And bad'st me bury love.

by your help and holy medicine. I bear no hatred, blessed man. For as you can see, my request also helps my enemy.

Friar Lawrence Good son, speak plainly and simply. Confessing in riddles brings riddles for absolution.

Romeo Then you must plainly know that rich Capulet's lovely daughter is my heart's desire. As my love is hers, so is hers mine. We are combined, except for what you must combine in holy marriage. When, where, and how we met, wooed, and exchanged vows—I'll tell you that as we walk. But I beg you to agree to marry us today.

Friar Lawrence Holy Saint Francis! What a change this is! Has Rosaline, whom you loved so dearly, been forgotten so quickly? Then young men's love doesn't truly lie in their hearts, but in their eyes. By Jesus and Mary, what a quantity of salt water has wet your yellow cheeks for love of Rosaline! How much salt water was wasted, giving flavor to a love that was never tasted! The sun hasn't yet burned off the vapor from your sighs. Your old groans still ring in my ancient ears. Look, there's still a stain on your cheek from an old tear that hasn't been washed off yet. If you were ever *you* and these sorrows were yours, you and your sorrows were all devoted to Rosaline. And you've changed? Repeat this sentence, then: "Women fall from grace when men have no strength."

Romeo You often scolded me for loving Rosaline.

Friar Lawrence For doting on her, not for loving her, my pupil.

Romeo And you told me to bury my love.

Friar Lawrence   Not in a grave
    To lay one in, another out to have.

Romeo I pray thee chide me not. Her I love now
90   Doth grace for grace and love for love allow;
    The other did not so.

Friar Lawrence   O, she knew well
    Thy love did read by rote that could not spell.
    But, come young waverer, come go with me,
95   In one respect I'll thy assistant be;
    For this alliance may so happy prove
    To turn your households' rancour to pure love.

Romeo O, let us hence; I stand on sudden haste.

Friar Lawrence Wisely and slow; they stumble that run fast.

[Exeunt]

Friar Lawrence   Not to put one into a grave so you could take another one out.

Romeo   Please don't scold me. The girl I love now returns joy for joy and love for love. The other didn't.

Friar Lawrence   Oh, she knew your love just repeated what it heard and couldn't come up with words of its own. But come, young waverer, come along with me. There's one reason I'll assist you: This marriage could have the happy result of turning your families' hatred into pure love.

Romeo   Oh, let's go. I can't wait any longer!

Friar Lawrence   Wisely and slowly. Those who run fast, stumble.

[**Friar Lawrence** *and* **Romeo** *exit*]

Act II

Scene IV

A street. Enter **Benvolio** *and* **Mercutio**

Mercutio Where the devil should this Romeo be?
Came he not home tonight?

Benvolio Not to his father's. I spoke with his man.

Mercutio Why, that same pale hard-hearted wench, that
5 Rosaline, torments him so that he will sure run mad.

Benvolio Tybalt, the kinsman to old Capulet, hath sent a
letter to his father's house.

Mercutio A challenge, on my life.

Benvolio Romeo will answer it.

10 **Mercutio** Any man that can write may answer a letter.

Benvolio Nay, he will answer the letter's master, how he
dares, being dared.

Mercutio Alas, poor Romeo, he is already dead: stabbed with
a white wench's black eye; run through the ear with a love-
15 song; the very pin of his heart cleft with the blind bow-boy's
butt-shaft. And is he a man to encounter Tybalt?

Benvolio Why, what is Tybalt?

Mercutio More than Prince of Cats. O, he's the courageous
captain of compliments. He fights as you sing prick-song;
20 keeps time, distance, and proportion; he rest his minim rests,

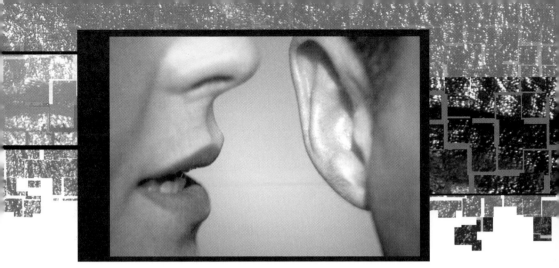

A street. **Benvolio** *and* **Mercutio** *enter.*

Mercutio Where the devil can this Romeo be? Didn't he come home last night?

Benvolio Not to his father's. I spoke to his servant.

Mercutio Why, that same pale, hard-hearted woman, that Rosaline, torments him so much he's bound to go mad.

Benvolio Old Capulet's nephew, Tybalt, sent a letter to Romeo's father's house.

Mercutio I'd bet my life it's a challenge to fight.

Benvolio Romeo will answer it.

Mercutio Any man who can write can answer a letter.

Benvolio No, I mean he'll answer the letter-writer by accepting his challenge. He'll show how he'll take on a dare.

Mercutio Alas, poor Romeo, he's already dead. Stabbed with a glance from that white woman's black eye, stabbed through the ear with a love song. Blind Cupid's toy arrow has stuck the very bull's-eye of his heart. And is he a man to fight with Tybalt?

Benvolio Why, what's so frightening about Tybalt?

Mercutio He's more than just the Prince of Cats. Oh, he's the courageous captain of fine points. He fights like you'd sing a note-perfect song: He keeps perfectly accurate time, pace, and rhythm. He takes his short rests—one, two, and the third is a

one, two and the third in your bosom; the very butcher of a
silk button, a duellist, a duellist; a gentleman of the very first
house, of the first and second cause. Ah, the immortal
passado! The punto reverso! The hay –

25 **Benvolio** The what?

Mercutio The pox of such antic, lisping, affecting
fantasticoes; these new tuners of accent! 'By Jesu, a very good
blade! A very tall man! A very good whore!' Why, is not this
a lamentable thing, grandsire, that we should be thus afflicted
30 with these strange flies, these fashion-mongers, these pardon
me's, who stand so much on the new form that they cannot
sit at ease on the old bench? O, their bones, their bones!

[*Enter* **Romeo**]

Benvolio Here comes Romeo, here comes Romeo.

Mercutio Without his roe, like a dried herring. O flesh, flesh,
35 how art thou fishified! Now is he for the numbers that
Petrarch flowed in. Laura, to his lady, was a kitchen-wench –
marry, she had a better love to berhyme her; Dido, a dowdy;
Cleopatra, a gipsy; Helen and Hero, hildings and harlots;
Thisbe, a gray eye or so, but not to the purpose. Signior
40 Romeo, bon jour! There's a French salutation to your French
slop. You gave us the counterfeit fairly last night.

Romeo Good morrow to you both. What counterfeit did I give
you?

Mercutio The slip, sir, the slip. Can you not conceive?

45 **Romeo** Pardon, good Mercutio; my business was great, and
in such a case as mine a man may strain courtesy.

Mercutio That's as much as to say, such a case as yours
constrains a man to bow in the hams.

sword thrust in your chest. He slices through silk shirt buttons like a butcher. A duelist, a duelist, a gentleman of the top school of fencing, well drilled in all its codes. Ah, the immortal forward thrust! The backhanded stroke! The thrust through—

Benvolio The what?

Mercutio The plague take these silly, accented, affected show-offs; these makers of fashionable phrases! "By Jesus, a very good blade! A bold fine fellow! A very good whore!" Well, old codger, isn't this a sorry thing, that we should be afflicted with these foreign parasites? These fashion-mongers, these pardon-me types, who stand by the new trends so much they can't sit easily on an old bench? Oh, their bones, their French *bons*!

  [**Romeo** *enters*]

Benvolio Here comes Romeo, here comes Romeo!

Mercutio Thin and spent, like a dried herring. Oh flesh, oh flesh, how fishified you are! Now he's ready for the verses that flowed from Petrarch's pen. Compared to his lady, Laura was a kitchen maid (though, truly, Laura had a better lover-poet to put her into rhymes), Dido was dowdy, Cleopatra was a gypsy, Helen and Hero were good-for-nothing loose women. Thisbe had gray eyes or something, but nothing worth mentioning. Signor Romeo, bonjour! There's a French greeting for your French-styled pants. You gave a counterfeit deal last night.

Romeo Good day to you both. What deal did I give you?

Mercutio The slip, sir, the slip! Can't you follow me?

Romeo I'm sorry, good Mercutio. My business was important, and in a case like mine a man may bend the rules of courtesy.

Mercutio That's like saying that a case like yours forces a man to bend from bow legs.

Romeo Meaning to curtsy.

50 **Mercutio** Thou hast most kindly hit it.

Romeo A most courteous exposition.

Mercutio Nay, I am the very pink of courtesy.

Romeo Pink for flower.

Mercutio Right.

55 **Romeo** Why, then is my pump well flowered.

Mercutio Sure wit! Follow me this jest now till thou hast worn out thy pump, that, when the single sole of it is worn, the jest may remain, after the wearing, solely singular.

Romeo O single-soled jest, solely singular for the singleness!

60 **Mercutio** Come between us, good Benvolio; my wits faints.

Romeo Swits and spurs, swits and spurs; or I'll cry a match.

Mercutio Nay, if our wits run the wild-goose chase, I am done; for thou hast more of the wild goose in one of thy wits than, I am sure, I have in my whole five. Was I with you there
65 for the goose?

Romeo Thou wast never with me for anything when thou wast not there for the goose.

Mercutio I will bite thee by the ear for that jest.

Romeo Nay, good goose, bite not.

70 **Mercutio** Thy wit is a very bitter sweeting; it is most sharp sauce.

Romeo And is it not then well served in to a sweet goose?

Mercutio O, here's a wit of cheveril, that stretches from an inch narrow to an ell broad!

Romeo Meaning to curtsy?

Mercutio Now you've hit it.

Romeo Very courteously said.

Mercutio Oh, indeed, I'm a paragon, the pink of courtesy.

Romeo "Pink" as in flower.

Mercutio Right.

Romeo Well, then, my shoe is very flowery, since it's been "pinked" with pinking shears.

Mercutio A steady wit! Let's keep this joke going until you've worn out that shoe. When that shoe's thin sole is worn out, the joke will outlast it and remain, solely singular.

Romeo Oh what a feeble, thin-soled joke, singular solely for its absurdity!

Mercutio Good Benvolio, break our contest up. My wits are tiring!

Romeo Whips and spurs! Bring it on! Or else I'll call the match.

Mercutio Well, if our wits play follow-the-leader in a wild-goose chase, I'm done. You've got more wild goose in one of your wits than I have in all five, I'm sure. Did I score a point just now with that bit about the "goose"?

Romeo There's always a bit of the goose, where you're concerned.

Mercutio I'll bite your ear for that joke.

Romeo No, good goose, don't bite.

Mercutio Your wit's as biting as a bitter apple. It's a very sharp sauce.

Romeo Isn't sharp applesauce what's served with a sweet goose?

Mercutio Oh, here's a kid-leather wit, that stretches from one-inch narrow to forty-five inches broad!

75 **Romeo** I stretch it out for that word 'broad', which, added to the goose, proves thee far and wide a broad goose.

Mercutio Why, is not this better now than groaning for love? Now art thou sociable, now art thou Romeo; now art thou what thou art by art as well as by nature; for this drivelling
80 love is like a great natural that runs lolling up and down to hide his bauble in a hole.

Benvolio Stop there, stop there.

Mercutio Thou desirest me to stop in my tale against the hair.

85 **Benvolio** Thou wouldst else have made thy tale large.

Mercutio O, thou art deceived: I would have made it short; for I was come to the whole depth of my tale, and meant, indeed, to occupy the argument no longer.

Romeo Here's goodly gear!

[*Enter* **Nurse** *and her man,* **Peter**]

90 **Mercutio** A sail, a sail!

Benvolio Two, two; a shirt and a smock.

Nurse Peter!

Peter Anon.

Nurse My fan, Peter.

95 **Mercutio** Good Peter, to hide her face; for her fan's the fairer face.

Nurse God ye good morrow, gentlemen.

Mercutio God ye good den, fair gentlewoman.

Nurse Is it good den?

Romeo I'll stretch it further to include that word "broad"—which, added to that broad joke about the goose, proves you're a big fat goose far and wide.

Mercutio Well, now, isn't this better than groaning over love? Now you're being sociable, now you're Romeo again. Now you are who you are by art as well as nature! This drivelling love is like a big idiot who runs up and down with his tongue hanging out, looking for a hole to hide his toy in.

Benvolio Stop there, stop there.

Mercutio You want me to stop short in telling my tale, against my wish?

Benvolio Otherwise your wish would have made your tale long.

Mercutio Oh, you're wrong. I would have made it short, since I'd gone as far into it as I could, and I meant, indeed, to pull out of the argument.

Romeo Here's a splendid outfit!

[*The* **Nurse** *and* **Peter,** *her servant, enter*]

Mercutio [*making fun of the Nurse's headdress and clothes*] A ship, a sailing ship!

Benvolio Two, two! A man's shirt and a woman's smock!

Nurse Peter!

Peter Coming.

Nurse Bring my fan, Peter.

Mercutio Good Peter, it's to hide her face. Her fan is a prettier face!

Nurse Good morning to you, gentlemen.

Mercutio Good afternoon to you, fair lady.

Nurse Is it afternoon?

100 **Mercutio** 'Tis no less, I tell ye; for the bawdy hand of the dial is now upon the prick of noon.

Nurse Out upon you! What a man are you?

Romeo One, gentlewoman, that God hath made himself to mar.

105 **Nurse** By my troth, it is well said. 'For himself to mar' quoth 'a! Gentlemen can any of you tell me where I may find the young Romeo?

Romeo I can tell you; but young Romeo will be older when you have found him than he was when you sought him. I am
110 the youngest of that name, for fault of a worse.

Nurse You say well.

Mercutio Yea, is the worst well? Very well too, i' faith; wisely, wisely.

Nurse If you be he, sir, I desire some confidence with you.

115 **Benvolio** She will indite him to some supper.

Mercutio A bawd, a bawd, a bawd! So, ho!

Romeo What hast thou found?

Mercutio No hare, sir; unless a hare, sir, in a lenten pie, that is something stale and hoar ere it be spent. [*He sings*]

120   An old hare hoar,
        And an old hare hoar,
     Is very good meat in Lent;
        But a hare that is hoar
        Is too much for a score,
125   When it hoars ere it be spent.

Romeo, will you come to your father's? We'll to dinner thither.

Mercutio It's no less than that. The bawdy hand of the clock touches noon, erect at the top of the dial.

Nurse Oh, go away! What kind of man are you?

Romeo One that God made to injure himself, gentle lady.

Nurse In faith, that's well said. "To injure himself," he said! Gentlemen, can any of you tell me where I can find the young Romeo?

Romeo I can tell you, but "young Romeo" will be older when you've found him than he was when you started looking. I am the youngest of that name, for lack of a worse.

Nurse Well put.

Mercutio Oh, so his "worse" is put well? Well, well; very well put, too. Indeed, very wise, very wise.

Nurse If you are he, sir, I'd like to confide with you. [*She means "I'd like to confer with you"*]

Benvolio [*Making fun of her misuse of words*] She'd like to "indite" him to dinner.

Mercutio A bawd, a bawd, a bawd! So, ho!

Romeo What have you found?

Mercutio Not a hare, sir. Unless it's a hare in a meager Lent pie, that's stale and moldy before it's done. [*He sings*]

> An old gray hare
> And an old gray hare
> Is very good Lenten meat,
> But a hare that's gray
> Isn't worth what you pay
> When it's gray before you eat.

Romeo, are you going to your father's? We'll have dinner there.

Romeo I will follow you.

Mercutio Farewell ancient lady. Farewell, lady, lady, lady.

[*Exeunt* **Mercutio** *and* **Benvolio**]

130 **Nurse** I pray you, sir, what saucy merchant was this that was
so full of his ropery?

Romeo A gentleman, nurse, that loves to hear himself talk,
and will speak more in a minute than he will stand to in a
month.

135 **Nurse** An 'a speak anything against me, I'll take him down,
and 'a were lustier than he is, and twenty such Jacks; and if I
cannot, I'll find those that shall. Scurvy knave! I am not of his
flirt-gills; I am none of his skains-mates. And thou must stand
by too, and suffer every knave to use me at his pleasure?

140 **Peter** I saw no man use you at his pleasure. If I had, my
weapon should quickly have been out, I warrant you. I dare
draw as soon as another man, if I see occasion in a good
quarrel, and the law on my side.

Nurse Now, afore God, I am so vexed that every part about
145 me quivers. Scurvy knave! Pray you sir, a word; and as I
told you, my young lady bid me enquire you out. What she
bid me say I will keep to myself. But first let me tell ye, if ye
should lead her in a fool's paradise, as they say, it were a
very gross kind of behaviour, as they say; for the gentle-
150 woman is young, and therefore, if you should deal double
with her, truly it were an ill thing to be offered to any gentlewoman, and very weak dealing.

Romeo Nurse, commend me to thy lady and mistress. I
protest unto thee –

155 **Nurse** Good heart, and i' faith I will tell her as much. Lord,
Lord! She will be a joyful woman.

Romeo I'll follow you.

Mercutio Farewell, ancient lady. Farewell, lady, lady, lady.

[**Mercutio** *and* **Benvolio** *exit*]

Nurse Tell me, sir, who was that saucy fellow who was so full of dirty jokes?

Romeo A gentleman, Nurse, who loves to hear himself talk. He'll talk more in a minute than he'll do in a month.

Nurse If he says anything bad about me, I'll take him down. I'll take on friskier men than he, twenty of them! And if I can't, I'll find those who will. Despicable villain! I'm not one of his loose women; I'm no low company! [*To* **Peter**] And you just stand there, letting every man take advantage of me?

Peter I didn't see any man take advantage of you. If I had, I guarantee I would have taken my weapon out quickly. I'll draw as soon as any man, if there's a chance of a good quarrel and the law's on my side.

Nurse Now, before God, I'm so upset that I'm quivering all over! Despicable villain! Please, sir, I'd like a word. As I told you, my young lady asked me to find where you were. What she told me to say, I'll keep to myself. But first, let me tell you that if you're leading her into a "fool's paradise," as they say, that would be a disgusting thing to do, as they say. For the lady is young. And therefore, if you're dealing double with her, that's a bad hand to deal to any lady and a very mean trick.

Romeo Nurse, give my regards to your lady and mistress. I solemnly swear to you—

Nurse Bless your heart! And indeed, I'll tell her so. Lord, lord! She'll be a joyful woman.

Romeo What wilt thou tell her, nurse? Thou dost not mark
    me.

Nurse I will tell her, sir, that you do protest. Which, as I take
160   it, is a gentlemanlike offer.

Romeo Bid her devise
    Some means to come to shrift this afternoon,
    And there she shall at Friar Lawrence' cell
    Be shrived and married. Here is for thy pains.

165 **Nurse** No, truly sir; not a penny.

Romeo Go to – I say you shall.

Nurse This afternoon, sir? Well, she shall be there.

Romeo And stay, good nurse – behind the abbey wall
    Within this hour my man shall be with thee,
170   And bring thee cords made like a tackled stair,
    Which to the high top-gallant of my joy
    Must be my convoy in the secret night.
    Farewell, be trusty, and I'll quit thy pains.
    Farewell, commend me to thy mistress.

175 **Nurse** Now God in heaven bless thee! Hark you sir.

Romeo What say'st thou, my dear nurse?

Nurse Is your man secret? Did you ne'er hear say
    Two may keep counsel, putting one away?

Romeo I warrant thee my man's as true as steel.

180 **Nurse** Well, sir. My mistress is the sweetest lady – Lord,
    Lord! when 'twas a little prating thing! O, there is a nobleman
    in town, one Paris, that would fain lay knife aboard. But she,
    good soul, had as lief see a toad, a very toad, as see him. I
    anger her sometimes, and tell her that Paris is the properer
185   man. But, I'll warrant you, when I say so she looks as pale as
    any clout in the versal world. Doth not rosemary and Romeo
    begin both with a letter?

Romeo What will you tell her, Nurse? You're not listening to me.

Nurse I'll tell her, sir, that you "solemnly swear." Which, as I take it, is a gentlemanly proposal.

Romeo Tell her to find some way to go to confession this afternoon. And there she'll give confession and be married in Friar Lawrence's chamber. [*He tips her*] This is for your trouble.

Nurse No, truly, sir—not a penny.

Romeo No, I insist.

Nurse This afternoon, sir? Well, she'll be there.

Romeo Wait, good Nurse. Within an hour, my servant will meet you behind the abbey wall and bring you a rope ladder, which I'll use to convey me to the top of my joy in the dark of night. Farewell. Be reliable, and I'll reward you for it. Farewell; give my regards to your mistress.

Nurse Now, God in heaven bless you! Listen, sir.

Romeo What is it, dear Nurse?

Nurse Can your servant keep a secret? Haven't you heard it said that "two can keep a secret, as long as one's not there"?

Romeo I guarantee my servant's as true as steel.

Nurse Well, sir. My mistress is the sweetest lady—Lord, Lord! When she was a little prattling thing! Oh, there's a nobleman in town, named Paris, who'd love to press his claim. But she, good soul, would as soon see a toad, a very toad, as see him. I anger her sometimes by telling her that Paris is the handsomer man. But, I'll tell you, when I say that, she looks as pale as the whitest sheet in the whole wide world. Don't "rosemary" and "Romeo" begin with the same letter?

Romeo Ay, nurse. What of that? Both with an R.

Nurse Ah, mocker! That's the dog's name. R is for the – no, I
190   know it begins with some other letter. And she hath the
        prettiest sententious of it, of you and rosemary, that it would
        do you good to hear it.

Romeo Commend me to thy lady.

Nurse Ay, a thousand times. Peter!

195 **Peter** Anon.

Nurse Before and apace.

[*Exeunt*]

Romeo Yes, Nurse. What about it? Both start with an *R.*

Nurse Ah, you're making fun of me. That's the dog that goes "Rrrr." *R* is for the—no; I know it begins with some other letter. And she has the prettiest saying about it—about you and rosemary. It would do you good to hear it.

Romeo My regards to your lady.

Nurse Yes, a thousand times. Peter!

Peter Coming.

Nurse Go ahead. Quickly!

[*They exit*]

Act II

Scene V

Capulet's orchard. Enter **Juliet**

Juliet The clock struck nine when I did send the nurse;
In half an hour she promised to return.
Perchance she cannot meet him. That's not so.
O she is lame! Love's heralds should be thoughts,
5 Which ten times faster glide than the sun's beams
Driving back shadows over louring hills;
Therefore do nimble-pinioned doves draw Love,
And therefore hath the wind-swift Cupid wings.
Now is the sun upon the highmost hill
10 Of this day's journey; and from nine till twelve
Is three long hours, yet she is not come.
Had she affections and warm youthful blood,
She would be as swift in motion as a ball.
My words would bandy her to my sweet love,
15 And his to me.
But old folks – many feign as they were dead,
Unwieldy, slow, heavy, and pale as lead.

[*Enter* **Nurse** *and* **Peter**]

O God, she comes! O honey nurse, what news?
Hast thou met with him? Send thy man away.

20 **Nurse** Peter, stay at the gate.

[*Exit* **Peter**]

Capulet's orchard. **Juliet** *enters.*

Juliet The clock struck nine when I sent off the nurse. She promised to return in half an hour. Perhaps she can't find him. That's not so. Oh, she's slow! Love's messengers should be like thoughts, which glide ten times faster than when sunbeams push shadows off gloomy hills. That's why nimble-winged doves pull the chariot of Venus. That's why Cupid, who's as swift as the wind, has wings. Now the sun has reached the highest point in its daily journey, and from nine until noon is three long hours, but still she hasn't come. If she had feelings and youth's warm blood, she'd move as fast as a ball. My words would toss her to my sweet love, and his would toss her back to me. But old folks—many of them play dead. They're stiff, slow, heavy, and pale as lead.

[**Peter** *and the* **Nurse** *enter*]

Oh, God, she's here! Oh, sweet Nurse, what news? Did you find him? Send your servant away.

Nurse Peter, stay by the gate.

[**Peter** *exits*]

Juliet   Now, good sweet nurse – O Lord, why look'st thou sad?
　　Though news be sad, yet tell them merrily.
　　If good, thou shamest the music of sweet news
　　By playing it to me with so sour a face.

25　**Nurse**   I am aweary! Give me leave a while.
　　Fie, how my bones ache! What a jaunce have I had!

Juliet   I would thou hadst my bones and I thy news.
　　Nay, come, I pray thee, speak. Good, good nurse, speak!

Nurse   Jesu, what haste! Can you not stay a while?
30　Do you not see that I am out of breath?

Juliet   How art thou out of breath, when thou hast breath
　　To say to me that thou art out of breath?
　　The excuse that thou dost make in this delay
　　Is longer than the tale thou dost excuse.
35　Is thy news good or bad? Answer to that.
　　Say either, and I'll stay the circumstance.
　　Let me be satisfied, is't good or bad?

Nurse   Well, you have made a simple choice! You know not
　　how to choose a man. Romeo! No, not he. Though his face be
40　better than any man's, yet his leg excels all men's. And for a
　　hand, and a foot, and a body, though they be not to be talked
　　on, yet they are past compare. He is not the flower of
　　courtesy, but I'll warrant him as gentle as a lamb. Go thy
　　ways, wench, serve God. What, have you dined at home?

45　**Juliet**   No, no. But all this did I know before.
　　What says he of our marriage? What of that?

Nurse   Lord, how my head aches! What a head have I!
　　It beats as it would fall in twenty pieces.
　　My back a t'other side! Ah, my back, my back!
50　Beshrew your heart for sending me about
　　To catch my death with jauncing up and down!

Juliet   Now, good sweet Nurse—oh, Lord, why do you look so sad? If the news is bad, tell it merrily anyway. If it's good, you're ruining the music sweet news makes by playing it to me with such a sour-looking face.

Nurse   I'm tired! Let me be for a minute. Bother, how my bones ache! What a jolting journey I've had!

Juliet   I wish you had my bones and I had your news. Now, come, please speak. Good, good Nurse, speak!

Nurse   By Jesus, what haste! Can't you wait a minute? Don't you see I'm out of breath?

Juliet   How can you be out of breath, when you've got breath to tell me you're out of breath? The excuses you make for delaying take longer than the tale you aren't telling. Is your news good or bad? Answer me that. Say it's one or the other, and I'll wait for the details. Satisfy my curiosity: Is it good or bad?

Nurse   Well, you have made a foolish choice! You don't know how to choose a man. Romeo! No, not him. Though his face is better-looking than any man's, while his legs surpass all men's. And as for his hand, his foot, and his body—though they're nothing to talk about, they're still beyond comparison. He is not the perfect example of courtesy, but I'll maintain that he's as gentle as a lamb. Go along, girl, serve God. Now, did you eat at home?

Juliet   No, no. But I knew all this already. What does he say about our marriage? What about that?

Nurse   Lord, how my head aches! Oh, such a painful head! It's pulsing like it's about to break into twenty pieces. My back on the other side! Ah, my back, my back! Curse your heart for sending me all over to catch my death from jolting up and down!

Juliet I'faith, I am sorry that thou art not well.
Sweet, sweet, sweet nurse, tell me, what says my love?

Nurse Your love says like an honest gentleman, and a
55   courteous, and a kind, and a handsome, and I warrant, a
virtuous – Where is your mother?

Juliet Where is my mother? Why, she is within.
Where should she be? How oddly thou repliest!
'Your love says like an honest gentleman,
60   "Where is your mother?" '

Nurse   O God's lady dear!
Are you so hot? Marry, come up, I trow.
Is this the poultice for my aching bones?
Henceforward, do your messages yourself.

65 **Juliet** Here's such a coil! Come, what says Romeo?

Nurse Have you got leave to go to shrift to-day?

Juliet I have.

Nurse Then hie you hence to Friar Lawrence' cell.
There stays a husband to make you a wife.
70   Now comes the wanton blood up in your cheeks.
They'll be in scarlet straight at any news.
Hie you to church. I must another way
To fetch a ladder, by the which your love
Must climb a bird's nest soon when it is dark.
75   I am the drudge, and toil in your delight.
But you shall bear the burden soon at night.
Go. I'll to dinner. Hie you to the cell.

Juliet Hie to high fortune! Honest nurse, farewell!

[*Exeunt*]

Juliet I'm truly sorry you're not well. Sweet, sweet, sweet Nurse, tell me: What did my love say?

Nurse Your love says—like an honorable gentleman, and a courteous, kind, handsome, and, I'll be bound, a virtuous— [*She breaks off*] Where's your mother?

Juliet Where's my mother? Why, she's inside. Where else should she be? What an odd reply! "Your love says, like an honorable gentleman, 'Where's your mother?'"

Nurse Oh, by our dear Lady! Are you so impatient? Really now! Is this the medicine for my aching bones? From now on, take your messages yourself.

Juliet Oh, such a fuss! Come, what does Romeo say?

Nurse Do you have permission to go to confession today?

Juliet Yes.

Nurse Then hurry to Friar Lawrence's chamber. A husband waits there to make you a wife. Now the impetuous blood rises to your cheeks! They'll turn scarlet at any news. Hurry off to church. I have to go a different way, to fetch a ladder, so your lover can come for you after dark. I'm the drudge that works for your delight. But you'll bear the burden soon at night! Go. I'll go to dinner. Hurry off to the friar's chamber!

Juliet Hurry to good fortune! Honest Nurse, farewell!

[**Juliet** *and the* **Nurse** *exit*]

Act II

Scene VI

Friar Lawrence's cell. Enter **Friar Lawrence** *and* **Romeo**

Friar Lawrence So smile the heavens upon this holy act
That after-hours with sorrow chide us not!

Romeo Amen, amen! But come what sorrow can,
It cannot countervail the exchange of joy
5   That one short minute gives me in her sight.
Do thou but close our hands with holy words,
Then love-devouring death do what he dare.
It is enough I may but call her mine.

Friar Lawrence These violent delights have violent ends,
10   And in their triumph die; like fire and powder,
Which, as they kiss, consume. The sweetest honey
Is loathsome in his own deliciousness,
And in the taste confounds the appetite.
Therefore love moderately: long love doth so;
15   Too swift arrives as tardy as too slow.

[*Enter* **Juliet**]

Here comes the lady. O, so light a foot
Will ne'er wear out the everlasting flint.
A lover may bestride the gossamer
That idles in the wanton summer air
20   And yet not fall, so light is vanity.

Juliet Good even to my ghostly confessor.

Friar Lawrence's chamber. **Friar Lawrence** *and* **Romeo** *enter.*

Friar Lawrence May heaven smile upon this holy act and not punish it with sorrow later!

Romeo Amen, amen! But whatever sorrow comes, it can't measure against the joy that comes from seeing her for one short minute. If you will only join our hands in holy matrimony, then love-devouring death can do whatever he dares. For me, it's enough just to call her mine.

Friar Lawrence These violent joys have violent ends and die at the height of their strength. They're like fire and gunpowder, which are used up the moment they kiss. The sweetest honey can make you sick with its deliciousness and can kill the appetite when it's tasted. Therefore, love moderately. That's how love lasts. When people are too hasty, they come up just as short as those who are too slow.

[**Juliet** *enters*]

Here comes the lady. Oh, such a light-footed walk will never wear out the everlasting path! Lovers can walk along the spiderwebs that hang in the summer air and still not fall. So light are the world's brief joys.

Juliet Good evening, father confessor.

Friar Lawrence Romeo shall thank thee, daughter, for us both.

Juliet As much to him, else is his thanks too much.

25 **Romeo** Ah Juliet, if the measure of thy joy
    Be heaped like mine, and that thy skill be more
    To blazon it, then sweeten with thy breath
    This neighbour air, and let rich music's tongue
    Unfold the imagined happiness that both
30   Receive in either by this dear encounter.

Juliet Conceit, more rich in matter than in words,
    Brags of his substance, not of ornament.
    They are but beggars that can count their worth;
    But my true love is grown to such excess
35   I cannot sum up sum of half my wealth.

Friar Lawrence Come, come with me, and we will make short work.
    For, by your leaves, you shall not stay alone
    Till holy church incorporate two in one.

[Exeunt]

Friar Lawrence Romeo will thank you, daughter, for both of us.

[**Romeo** *kisses her*]

Juliet I'll return as much thanks to him [*she kisses him back*], or else he's given too much.

Romeo Ah, Juliet! If the scale of your joy is as great as mine, and if your ability to speak about it is better, then sweeten the neighboring air with your breath: Let the rich music of your speech describe the unspoken mutual happiness that will come from our dear meeting!

Juliet Imagination finds more glory in rich reality than in fancy phrases. Those who can count their wealth are beggars. But my true love has grown so vast that I can't sum up the half of my riches.

Friar Lawrence Come, come with me, and we'll finish this work quickly. For, begging your pardons, you can't be left alone until the Holy Church joins the two of you as one.

[*They exit*]

Comprehension   **Check What You Know**

1. What do you learn from the Chorus?

2. Describe the conversation between Romeo and Juliet in Scene 2. What brings them joy? What brings them sorrow?

3. At what time of day do Romeo and Juliet speak in Scene 2? Why do they meet at this time? How does the time of day fit the mood of their meeting?

4. What role does Friar Lawrence play for Romeo and Juliet?

5. How does the Nurse influence the events of Act 2?

6. How do Mercutio and Benvolio describe Romeo's actions in Scene 1?

7. What does Romeo learn from the Nurse?

8. Describe Juliet's role in Act 2. At which points does she wait for events to unfold for her? When does she take action on her own? How would you describe her strengths and weaknesses?

Activities & Role-Playing   **Classes or Book Clubs**

Highs and Lows The balcony scene in Act 2 is one of the most famous scenes in theater. Take the parts of Romeo and Juliet and role-play Scene 2. Imagine the danger that Romeo is in and the physical positions of the pair as they speak. Consider Juliet's fear for Romeo's life. With such physical effort, fear, and excitement, the lines between Romeo and Juliet might sound breathy— and perhaps hurried.

Laura Hicks as Juliet and Derek D. Smith as Romeo in The Shakespeare Theatre's production of *Romeo and Juliet* directed by Michael Kahn. Photo by Joan Marcus.

Outfitting the Friar Make a list of props and clothing for Friar Lawrence's character. Refer to religious references or the Internet for ideas. Then make a chart listing the importance of each prop. Note how each prop contributes to the action of Act 2. Show how each prop indicates an aspect of Friar Lawrence's character or personality.

Discussion Classes or Book Clubs

1. Review each set of the following lines by Juliet in Scene 2. Discuss each set of lines and their meaning.

   O Romeo, Romeo, wherefore art thou Romeo?
   Deny thy father and refuse thy name.
   And I'll no longer be a Capulet. (lines 35–37)

   My bounty is boundless as the sea,
   My love as deep; the more I give to thee
   The more I have, for both are infinite. (lines 138–140)

2. How do the adults (such as Friar Lawrence and the Nurse) in Act 2 affect Romeo and Juliet's relationship? How much do Romeo and Juliet rely on others?

Suggestions for Writing Improve Your Skills

1. Write an additional scene for Act 2. Have the Nurse speaking in the Capulet home with one of her friends—such as another servant. What might she tell him or her? What opinion might she have of Romeo and Juliet's love for each other? How might she like or dislike helping Juliet?

2. Write a poem or some lines of dialogue that compare some person you know to a thing. Who is like a river, like the moon, like a mountain, like a sturdy house? Who is like a migrating, singing, hunting, nesting, or fledgling bird? Who is like an eagle, like a swan, or like an owl? What specific details help you describe the person's resemblance to what they are being compared to?

All the World's a Stage Introduction

In less than two days, Romeo and Juliet have met, flirted, and married—without so much as a dinner date squeezed in between these events. No wonder Friar Lawrence worries about them!

Like most young lovers, Romeo and Juliet live intensely in the moment. To fit those moments, Shakespeare sets his scenes during vividly specific times of day that fit the action especially well. For example, the play's very first scene takes place in the morning, when the sun brings out the hot tempers. But in the secret, half-lit time between sunset and dawn, love blooms in soft-spoken privacy. For Romeo and Juliet, each hour is a little world, all on its own.

What's in a Name? Characters

Until now, both the Montague and Capulet families have stayed "behind the scenes," although their influence has been felt—and not always for the good. Now Juliet's parents will begin to take an active interest in her love life. You may even learn why Juliet turns for help not to her *real* father but to her father-confessor, Friar Lawrence.

We'll see much more in Act 3 of the relationships between Juliet and her parents and between Capulet and Lady Capulet. According to the laws of the time, such relationships were very clear cut. Legally, man ruled woman and parent ruled child—period. How well do the Capulets fit this model? How different are things today?

Another member of the Capulet clan is Tybalt, Juliet's cousin. In Act 1, we saw Tybalt's hot temper. Later, we learned of his dangerous skills with a sword. With Tybalt around, it seems unlikely that the Capulets can stay out of trouble with their sovereign, Prince Escalus. Meanwhile, two of the prince's relatives, Mercutio and Count Paris, are getting more involved in the feud.

COME WHAT MAY Things to Watch For

Night and day. Black and white. Romeo and Juliet. Three "couples"— three sets of opposites. *Romeo and Juliet*'s language is full of such couplings. In the play's very first scene, Romeo complained about the "brawling love" and "loving hate" he felt for Rosaline. When he met Juliet, his beloved enemy, this strange pairing of opposites (called *oxymoron*) became more than words. In a way, Romeo became the victim of the ultimate "poetic justice"—forced to live out the literal meaning of his fancy phrases!

In Act 3, watch for more oxymoronic language that expresses the lovers' tricky situation. When you've fallen in love, did you pick someone just like you? Or was your soul mate also your opposite?

All Our Yesterdays Historical and Social Context

Many aspects of Shakespeare's life remain a mystery. But we do have a copy of "Will" Shakespeare's will. He left most of his estate to Susana, the elder of his two daughters. Not long before he died, he changed his will to make sure his daughter Judith's husband—who was a slippery character—couldn't run off with all of Judith's dowry funds. Dowries were gifts of cash and/or property that were transferred from the bride's to the groom's family at marriage. In general, wives had no property of their own: all their assets went to their husbands when they married.

The Play's the Thing Staging

Imagine you're watching a big-budget movie, full of extras, special effects, and scenic locations. Now imagine you're a little boy or girl playing make-believe in your room. Which is closer to Shakespeare?

Given the chance to go back in time to watch *Romeo and Juliet*'s first performances, some time travelers might be very disappointed. After all, there were no elaborate changes of lighting or scenery. The Tiring House at the back of the stage could be used as Juliet's balcony, the house fronts lining a public street, and the inside of the Capulets' house. Low-tech, indeed—but how flexible! Suppose you were Shakespeare, working with a small company of actors playing multiple roles. How many could you spare for a crowd scene? How could you use the doors at the back of the stage to help your audience remember which actors are Capulets and which are Montagues?

Shakespeare often used dialogue "clues" to help his audience picture time of day, scenery, and location. Notice how frequently his characters mention the time and place in which the action is set. Shakespeare is quite subtle in providing this information without interrupting the natural "flow" of the action.

My Words Fly Up Language

In Act 3's second scene, Juliet makes a string of puns that play with the words *I, eye,* and *ay.* You might say she exchanges an "eye" for an "I." If that last pun left you groaning, you may also find yourself struggling with Juliet's puns at what may seem like a very inappropriate moment. Shakespeare's puns aren't always comic. On some occasions, they may be used to show a character's confusion or distress. They frequently point to the play's deeper themes.

In Act 3, Scene 1, some wordplay involving the word *man* occurs. *Man* meant both "mature male" and "male servant." Watch for ideas of "manhood" throughout the play, especially as they apply to the teenage hero, Romeo. What does it mean to be a "real man"?

Act III

Scene I

Enter **Mercutio, Benvolio** *and* **Men**

Benvolio   I pray thee, good Mercutio, let's retire;
The day is hot, the Capels are abroad,
And if we meet we shall not 'scape a brawl,
For now these hot days is the mad blood stirring.

5 **Mercutio**   Thou art like one of these fellows that, when he
enters the confines of a tavern, claps me his sword upon the
table and says 'God send me no need of thee!' and by the
operation of the second cup draws him on the drawer, when
indeed there is no need.

10 **Benvolio**   Am I like such a fellow?

Mercutio   Come, come, thou art as hot a Jack in thy mood as
any in Italy; and as soon moved to be moody, and as soon
moody to be moved.

Benvolio   And what to?

15 **Mercutio**   Nay, and there were two such, we should have none
shortly, for one would kill the other. Thou? Why, thou wilt
quarrel with a man that hath a hair more or a hair less in his
beard than thou hast. Thou wilt quarrel with a man for
cracking nuts, having no other reason but because thou hast
20   hazel eyes. What eye but such an eye would spy out such a
quarrel? Thy head is as full of quarrels as an egg is full of
meat, and yet thy head hath been beaten as addle as an egg for
quarrelling. Thou hast quarrelled with a man for coughing in

Mercutio, Benvolio, *and* **Servants** *enter.*

Benvolio Please, good Mercutio, let's go home. The day is hot, and the Capulets are out. If we meet them, we won't escape a fight. These hot days make angry blood stir.

Mercutio You're like one of these fellows who, when he enters a tavern, slams his sword on the table and says, "May God not let me need you." By the time he's had his second drink, he draws his sword on the barkeeper, although there's no need!

Benvolio Am I a fellow like that?

Mercutio Come, come! You are as hot-blooded a fellow when you're angry as anybody in Italy. You're as soon as anyone to be moved, and as easily moved as anyone.

Benvolio And what to?

Mercutio [*pretending he thinks "to" meant "two"*] Oh, no! If there were two like you, we'd quickly have none of you, for one would kill the other. You? Why, you'd quarrel with a man about whether he has a hair more or a hair less in his beard than you have. You'd quarrel with a man for cracking a nut, for no reason but that you have hazel eyes. Whose eye but one like yours would find a quarrel with that? Your head is as full of quarrels as an egg is full of food, but your head has been as beaten as a scrambled egg for your quarreling. You've

the street, because he hath wakened thy dog that hath lain
25   asleep in the sun. Didst thou not fall out with a tailor for
wearing his new doublet before Easter; with another for tying
his new shoes with old riband? And yet thou wilt tutor me
from quarrelling!

Benvolio And I were so apt to quarrel as thou art, any man
30   should buy the fee simple of my life for an hour and a quarter.

Mercutio The fee simple! O simple!

[*Enter* **Tybalt** *and others*]

Benvolio By my head, here come the Capulets.

Mercutio By my heel, I care not.

Tybalt Follow me close, for I will speak to them.
35   Gentlemen, good e'en: a word with one of you.

Mercutio And but one word with one of us? Couple it with
something, make it a word and a blow.

Tybalt You shall find me apt enough to that, sir, and you will
give me occasion.

40 **Mercutio** Could you not take some occasion without giving?

Tybalt Mercutio, thou consortest with Romeo.

Mercutio Consort? What, dost thou make us minstrels? And
thou make minstrels of us, look to hear nothing but discords.
Here's my fiddlestick, here's that shall make you dance.
45   Zounds, consort!

Benvolio We talk here in the public haunt of men.
Either withdraw unto some private place,
Or reason coldly of your grievances,
Or else depart. Here all eyes gaze on us.

quarreled with a man for coughing in the street because he woke up your dog that was asleep in the sun. Didn't you quarrel with a tailor for wearing his new jacket before Easter, and with someone else for tying his new shoes with an old ribbon? And yet you'll talk to me about quarreling?

Benvolio   If I were as likely to quarrel as you are, a man could buy my life for an hour and a quarter—with absolute ownership, that is, with fee simple.

Mercutio   "Fee simple"? How simple!

[**Tybalt** *and others enter*]

Benvolio   By my head, here come the Capulets.

Mercutio   By my heel, I don't care!

Tybalt   [*to his followers*] Stay close behind me. I'll speak to them. [*To* **Benvolio** *and* **Mercutio**] Gentlemen, good evening. A word with one of you.

Mercutio   Just one word with just one of us? Add something else: Make it a word and a blow.

Tybalt   You'll find me happy enough to do that, sir. Just give me a reason.

Mercutio   Couldn't you make a reason, without being given one?

Tybalt   Mercutio—you belong to Romeo's group—

Mercutio   Group? What! Do you think we're musicians? Make musicians of us and you'll hear nothing but discords. Here's my fiddlestick—a sword. That'll make you dance. By God's wounds! Group!

Benvolio   We're talking here in the public street. Either let's go someplace private, or discuss your disagreements calmly, or let's leave. Here, all eyes are watching us.

50   **Mercutio**   Men's eyes were made to look, and let them gaze.
      I will not budge for no man's pleasure, I.

[*Enter* **Romeo**]

Tybalt   Well, peace be with you, sir, here comes my man.

Mercutio   But I'll be hanged, sir, if he wear your livery.
      Marry, go before to field, he'll be your follower.
55   Your worship in that sense may call him 'man'.

Tybalt   Romeo, the love I bear thee can afford
      No better term than this: thou art a villain.

Romeo   Tybalt, the reason that I have to love thee
      Doth much excuse the appertaining rage
60   To such a greeting: villain am I none,
      Therefore farewell. I see thou knowest me not.

Tybalt   Boy, this shall not excuse the injuries
      That thou hast done me, therefore turn and draw.

Romeo   I do protest I never injured thee,
65   But love thee better than thou canst devise
      Till thou shalt know the reason of my love.
      And so, good Capulet, which name I tender
      As dearly as mine own, be satisfied.

Mercutio   O calm, dishonourable, vile submission:
70   Alla stoccata carries it away! [*He draws*]
      Tybalt, you rat-catcher, will you walk?

Tybalt   What wouldst thou have with me?

Mercutio   Good King of Cats, nothing but one of your nine
      lives that I mean to make bold withal, and as you shall use me
75   hereafter, dry-beat the rest of the eight. Will you pluck your
      sword out of his pilcher by the ears? Make haste, lest mine be
      about your ears ere it be out.

Mercutio   Men's eyes were made to look, so let them stare. I won't budge to please anyone. Not I.

[**Romeo** *enters*]

Tybalt   Well, peace be with you, sir. Here comes my man.

Mercutio   I'll be damned, sir, if he'll wear the colors of your "man" servant! Why, to be sure, if you go to a dueling-field he'll go there with you. In that worthy sense, "Your Worship," you may call him your "man."

Tybalt   Romeo, I have so little love for you that I have nothing better to say than this: You're a villain!

Romeo   Tybalt, I have a reason to love you, and that keeps me from being angry at your greeting: I'm not a villain. So good-bye. I see you don't know me.

Tybalt   You "boy"! That's not an excuse for the insulting things you've done to me. So turn and draw.

Romeo   I'm telling you I've never done anything to harm you. I love you better than you can imagine—until you know the reason for my love. And so, good Capulet—a name I hold as dearly as my own—be satisfied.

Mercutio   What a calm, dishonorable, vile answer! The best fencer wins! Tybalt, you rat-catcher, will you step over here?

Tybalt   What do you want with me?

Mercutio   Good King of Cats, I only want one of your nine lives. And if you treat me badly in the future, I'll beat the rest of your eight lives. Will you pull your sword out of its scabbard by the ears? Hurry up—or my sword will have cut off your ears before your sword is out.

Tybalt I am for you. [*He draws*]

Romeo Gentle Mercutio, put thy rapier up.

80 **Mercutio** Come sir, your passado. [*They fight*]

Romeo Draw, Benvolio, beat down their weapons.
Gentlemen, for shame, forbear this outrage.
Tybalt! Mercutio! The Prince expressly hath
Forbid this bandying in Verona streets.
85 Hold, Tybalt! Good Mercutio!

[**Tybalt** *under* **Romeo**'s *arm thrusts* **Mercutio** *in*]

[*Exit* **Tybalt** *with his followers*]

Mercutio I am hurt.
A plague o' both your houses. I am sped.
Is he gone, and hath nothing?

Benvolio   What, art thou hurt?

90 **Mercutio** Ay, ay, a scratch, a scratch. Marry, 'tis enough.
Where's my page? Go villain, fetch a surgeon.

[*Exit* **Page**]

Romeo Courage man, the hurt cannot be much.

Mercutio No, 'tis not so deep as a well, nor so wide as a church
door, but 'tis enough, 'twill serve. Ask for me tomorrow and
95 you shall find me a grave man. I am peppered, I warrant, for
this world. A plague o' both your houses. Zounds, a dog, a
rat, a mouse, a cat, to scratch a man to death. A braggart, a
rogue, a villain, that fights by the book of arithmetic – why the
devil came you between us? I was hurt under your arm.

Tybalt I'm ready for you. [*He draws his sword*]

Romeo Gentle Mercutio! Put away your sword!

Mercutio Come sir, show me your best stroke! [**Tybalt** *and* **Mercutio** *fight*]

Romeo Draw, Benvolio. Force them to drop their weapons. Gentlemen, for shame! Stop this outrage. Tybalt! Mercutio! The Prince has expressly forbidden this fighting in Verona's streets. Stop, Tybalt! Good Mercutio!

[**Tybalt** *thrusts under* **Romeo's** *arm and wounds* **Mercutio**]

[**Tybalt** *and his followers exit*]

Mercutio I'm hurt. May a plague strike both your houses! I'm finished. Is he gone? Without a scratch?

Benvolio Are you hurt?

Mercutio Yes, yes, a scratch, a scratch. To be sure, it's enough. Where's my page? Go, fellow, get a doctor.

[*The* **Page** *exits*]

Romeo Courage, man. The wound can't be that bad.

Mercutio No, it's not as deep as a well or as wide as a church door, but it's enough. It will do. Look for me tomorrow, and you'll find me a "grave" man. I'm done for, I swear, for this world. May a plague strike both your houses! By God's wounds, a dog, a rat, a mouse, a cat, to scratch a man to death. A braggart, a rogue, a villain that fights by the duelist's book! Why the devil did you come between us? I was hurt by a strike that came underneath your arm.

100 **Romeo** I thought all for the best.

Mercutio Help me into some house, Benvolio,
Or I shall faint. A plague o' both your houses,
They have made worms' meat of me.
I have it, and soundly too. Your houses!

[*Exit* **Mercutio** *with* **Benvolio**]

105 **Romeo** This gentleman, the Prince's near ally,
My very friend, hath got this mortal hurt
In my behalf – my reputation stained
With Tybalt's slander – Tybalt that an hour
Hath been my cousin. O sweet Juliet,
110 Thy beauty hath made me effeminate
And in my temper softened valour's steel.

[*Enter* **Benvolio**]

Benvolio O Romeo, Romeo, brave Mercutio is dead.
That gallant spirit hath aspired the clouds
Which too untimely here did scorn the earth.

115 **Romeo** This day's black fate on more days doth depend:
This but begins the woe others must end.

[*Enter* **Tybalt**]

Benvolio Here comes the furious Tybalt back again.

Romeo Alive, in triumph, and Mercutio slain.
Away to heaven respective lenity,
120 And fire-eyed fury be my conduct now!
Now Tybalt, take the 'villain' back again
That late thou gav'st me, for Mercutio's soul
Is but a little way above our heads,
Staying for thine to keep him company.
125 Either thou, or I, or both must go with him.

Romeo I thought it was the best thing to do.

Mercutio Help me into a house, Benvolio, or I'll faint. May a plague strike both your houses! They've made worms' meat of me. I've had it, and thoroughly, too. Your houses!

[**Mercutio** *exits with* **Benvolio**]

Romeo This gentleman—the Prince's close relation, my true friend—got this mortal wound on my behalf—because Tybalt slandered my good name. Tybalt, who for just an hour has been my relative! Oh sweet Juliet, your beauty has made me unmanly and has softened the steel of courage in my nature.

[**Benvolio** *enters*]

Benvolio Oh Romeo, Romeo! Brave Mercutio is dead! His gallant spirit has risen to heaven, and he—much too young— has left the earth.

Romeo This day's dark fate will hang over the days to come. This is just the beginning of the days of sorrow that later days will end.

[**Tybalt** *enters*]

Benvolio Here comes the hotheaded Tybalt back again.

Romeo Alive, in triumph, and Mercutio dead! To heaven with considerate gentleness! Fire-eyed anger will be my guide now! Now Tybalt! Take back the "villain" insult that you just gave me. Mercutio's soul is just above our heads, waiting for yours to keep him company. Either you, or I, or both of us must go with him!

Tybalt Thou wretched boy, that didst consort him here,
     Shalt with him hence.

Romeo   This shall determine that.

                         [*They fight.* **Tybalt** *falls*]

Benvolio Romeo, away, be gone,
130   The citizens are up, and Tybalt slain!
     Stand not amazed. The Prince will doom thee death
     If thou art taken. Hence, be gone, away!

Romeo O, I am fortune's fool.

Benvolio   Why dost thou stay?

                              [*Exit* **Romeo**]

     [*Enter* **Citizens**]

135 **Citizen** Which way ran he that killed Mercutio?
     Tybalt, that murderer, which way ran he?

Benvolio There lies that Tybalt.

Citizen   Up, sir, go with me.
     I charge thee in the Prince's name obey.

     [*Enter* **Prince, Montague, Capulet,** *their* **Wives** *and all*]

140 **Prince** Where are the vile beginners of this fray?

Benvolio O noble Prince, I can discover all
     The unlucky manage of this fatal brawl.
     There lies the man, slain by young Romeo,
     That slew thy kinsman brave Mercutio.

Tybalt You wretched boy. You were one of his group here, and you'll go with him now.

Romeo This will decide that!

[*They fight.* **Tybalt** *is killed*]

Benvolio Romeo, get out of here! The people are coming! Tybalt's dead! Don't stand there in a daze. The Prince will condemn you to death if you're caught! Hurry, get out of here!

Romeo Oh, I'm fortune's plaything!

Benvolio Why do you stay?

[**Romeo** *exits*]

[*Some* **Citizens** *enter*]

Citizen Which way did Mercutio's killer run? Tybalt, that murderer, which way did he run?

Benvolio There lies Tybalt.

Citizen Get up, sir, go with me. In the Prince's name, I order you to obey.

[*The* **Prince, Montague, Capulet,** *their* **Wives,** *and others enter*]

Prince Where are the vile ones who started this fight?

Benvolio Oh noble Prince! I can give you all the unlucky details of this fatal fight. There lies the man—killed by young Romeo—who killed your relative, brave Mercutio.

145 **Lady Capulet** Tyblat, my cousin, O my brother's child!
O Prince, O husband, O, the blood is spilled
Of my dear kinsman. Prince, as thou art true,
For blood of ours shed blood of Montague.
O cousin, cousin!

150 **Prince** Benvolio, who began this bloody fray?

Benvolio Tybalt, here slain, whom Romeo's hand did slay.
Romeo, that spoke him fair, bid him bethink
How nice the quarrel was, and urged withal
Your high displeasure. All this uttered
155 With gentle breath, calm look, knees humbly bowed,
Could not take truce with the unruly spleen
Of Tybalt, deaf to peace, but that he tilts
With piercing steel at bold Mercutio's breast,
Who, all as hot, turns deadly point to point
160 And, with a martial scorn, with one hand beats
Cold death aside, and with the other sends
It back to Tybalt, whose dexterity
Retorts it. Romeo, he cries aloud
'Hold, friends! Friends part!' and swifter than his tongue
165 His agile arm beats down their fatal points
And twixt them rushes; underneath whose arm
An envious thrust from Tybalt hit the life
Of stout Mercutio; and then Tybalt fled,
But by and by comes back to Romeo,
170 Who had but newly entertained revenge,
And to't they go like lightning: for, ere I
Could draw to part them, was stout Tybalt slain,
And as he fell did Romeo turn and fly.
This is the truth, or let Benvolio die.

175 **Lady Capulet** He is a kinsman to the Montague.
Affection makes him false. He speaks not true.
Some twenty of them fought in this black strife
And all those twenty could but kill one life.
I beg for justice, which thou, Prince, must give.
180 Romeo slew Tybalt. Romeo must not live.

Lady Capulet Tybalt, my nephew! My brother's child! Oh Prince! Oh husband! Oh, the blood of my dear kinsman has been spilled! Prince, if you are just, for the blood of ours that has been shed, shed the blood of a Montague. Oh nephew, nephew!

Prince Benvolio, who began this bloody fight?

Benvolio Tybalt, lying dead here, who was killed by Romeo. Romeo spoke to him kindly, reminded him how unimportant the quarrel was, and urged him to think about how angry you would be. He said all this kindly, calmly, and on bended knee. Still he couldn't calm down the angry hostility of Tybalt, who was deaf to talk of peace. He thrusts his sword at bold Mercutio's chest. Just as angry, Mercutio draws his weapon as well. With the skill of a soldier, he defends himself from death with one hand and with the other hand sends death right back at Tybalt, who skillfully avoids it. Romeo shouts, "Stop, friends! Friends, break it up!" and faster than he speaks, he knocks aside their sword points and rushes between them. But Tybalt made a vicious strike under the arm of Romeo and struck the life of brave Mercutio. Then Tybalt ran. But he soon came back to Romeo, who only then thought of revenge. They began to fight with the speed of lightning. Before I could draw my sword to separate them, brave Tybalt was killed. And when he fell, Romeo turned and ran. This is the truth, I swear on my life.

Lady Capulet He is a relative of the Montague, Romeo. Affection makes him lie. He's not telling the truth. Some twenty of them fought in this evil fight, and all those twenty could only take one life. I beg for justice, which you must give, Prince. Romeo killed Tybalt. Romeo must not live.

Prince   Romeo slew him, he slew Mercutio.
Who now the price of his dear blood doth owe?

Montague   Not Romeo, Prince, he was Mercutio's friend.
His fault concludes but what the law should end,
185   The life of Tybalt.

Prince   And for that offence
Immediately we do exile him hence.
I have an interest in your hearts' proceeding;
My blood for your rude brawls doth lie a-bleeding.
190   But I'll amerce you with so strong a fine
That you shall all repent the loss of mine.
I will be deaf to pleading and excuses.
Nor tears nor prayers shall purchase out abuses.
Therefore, use none. Let Romeo hence in haste,
195   Else, when he is found, that hour is his last.
Bear hence this body, and attend our will.
Mercy but murders, pardoning those that kill.

[*Exeunt*]

Prince   Romeo killed Tybalt, Tybalt killed Mercutio. Who now pays the price of his death?

Montague   Not Romeo, Prince, he was Mercutio's friend. His fault was only that he ended what the law would have ended—the life of Tybalt.

Prince   And for that offense, we banish him immediately—he must leave Verona. I have a personal interest in your vengeful quarrel: My relative Mercutio lies dead because of your rough brawls. But I'll fine you so heavily that you'll be sorry for my loss. I won't hear your pleading and excuses. Neither tears nor prayers will buy your way out of these abuses. So don't use them. Let Romeo leave quickly, or else that hour when he is found will be his last. Take away this body, and come to hear my further judgment. Mercy only causes more murders, by encouraging others to kill.

[*They exit*]

Act III

Scene II

Juliet's room

[*Enter* **Juliet**]

Juliet Gallop apace, you fiery-footed steeds,
Towards Phoebus' lodging. Such a waggoner
As Phaeton would whip you to the west
And bring in cloudy night immediately.
5 Spread thy close curtain, love-performing night,
That runaway's eyes may wink, and Romeo
Leap to these arms untalked-of and unseen.
Lovers can see to do their amorous rite
By their own beauties; or, if love be blind,
10 It best agrees with night. Come, civil night,
Thou sober-suited matron, all in black,
And learn me how to lose a winning match
Played for a pair of stainless maidenhoods.
Hood my unmanned blood, bating in my cheeks,
15 With thy black mantle, till strange love grow bold,
Think true love acted simple modesty.
Come night, come Romeo, come thou day in night.
For thou wilt lie upon the wings of night
Whiter than new snow upon a raven's back.
20 Come gentle night, come loving black-browed night,
Give me my Romeo; and when he shall die
Take him and cut him out in little stars,
And he will make the face of heaven so fine

162

Juliet's room. **Juliet** *enters.*

Juliet Gallop speedily, you fiery-footed horses, pulling the chariot of the sun to its nightly resting place. A driver like Phaeton—the sun-god's son—could whip you toward the west and bring in the cloudy night immediately. Spread your concealing curtains, you love-bringing night, so those runaway horses' eyes may close. Romeo can then leap into these arms without being talked about or being seen. Lovers can see to make love by their own shining light. Or, if love is blind, it finds night most agreeable. Come, solemn night, you somberly-dressed matron, all in black. Teach me how to lose this match that we play with our virginities as stakes—that way I win by losing. Cover with your black cloak my untamed blood that flutters in my cheeks, until my shy love grows bold, and thinks that true love is an act of simple chastity. Come, night, come, Romeo! Come, you day of my night! You will stand out against the wings of night, whiter than new snow upon a raven's back. Come, gentle night, come loving, black-browed night! Give me my Romeo. And when he shall die, take him and cut him up into little stars. He will make the face of heaven so beautiful that all the world will be in love with

That all the world will be in love with night,
25 And pay no worship to the garish sun.
O, I have bought the mansion of a love
But not possessed it, and though I am sold,
Not yet enjoyed. So tedious is this day
As is the night before some festival
30 To an impatient child that hath new robes
And may not wear them. O, here comes my Nurse.

[*Enter* **Nurse** *with cords, wringing her hands*]

And she brings news, and every tongue that speaks
But Romeo's name speaks heavenly eloquence.
Now, Nurse, what news? What hast thou there?
35 The cords that Romeo bid thee fetch?

Nurse   Ay, ay, the cords.

Juliet Ay me, what news? Why dost thou wring thy hands?

Nurse Ah well-a-day, he's dead, he's dead, he's dead!
We are undone, lady, we are undone.
40 Alack the day, he's gone, he's killed, he's dead.

Juliet Can heaven be so envious?

Nurse   Romeo can,
Though heaven cannot. O Romeo, Romeo,
Who ever would have thought it? Romeo!

45 **Juliet** What devil art thou that dost torment me thus?
This torture should be roared in dismal hell.
Hath Romeo slain himself? Say thou but 'Ay'
And that bare vowel 'I' shall poison more
Than the death-darting eye of cockatrice.
50 I am not I if there be such an 'Ay'.
Or those eyes shut that makes thee answer 'Ay'.
If he be slain say 'Ay', or if not, 'No'.
Brief sounds determine of my weal or woe.

night and stop worshipping the glaring sun. Oh, I have bought a mansion called love, but I haven't yet occupied it! And though I've been sold, I haven't yet been enjoyed by my owner. This day seems to last so long. It's as long as the night before a festival seems to an impatient child who has new clothes and can't yet wear them. Oh, here comes my Nurse.

[*The **Nurse** enters with a rope ladder, wringing her hands*]

And she brings news. Every tongue that speaks Romeo's name speaks heavenly eloquence. Now, Nurse, what news? What do you have there? The ropes that Romeo asked you to bring?

Nurse Yes, yes, the ropes.

Juliet Oh dear, what's the news? Why are you wringing your hands?

Nurse Alas, he's dead, he's dead, he's dead! We're ruined, lady, we're ruined! Alas, he's gone! He's killed! He's dead!

Juliet Can heaven be so malicious?

Nurse Romeo can, though heaven can't! Oh Romeo, Romeo! Whoever would have thought it? Romeo!

Juliet What devil are you that you should torment me like this? This torture belongs in hopeless hell. Has Romeo killed himself? Just say "Ay" and that small vowel "I" will be more poisonous to me than the deadly eye of that legendary creature, the cockatrice, which killed with its look. I'll no longer be "I," if "Ay" is the answer, or if death has closed his eyes who makes you answer "Ay." If he is killed, say "Ay," or if not, say "No." These brief words will decide my happiness or misery.

Nurse I saw the wound, I saw it with mine eyes –
55   God save the mark – here on his manly breast.
        A piteous corse, a bloody piteous corse,
        Pale, pale as ashes, all bedaubed in blood –
        All in gore-blood. I swounded at the sight.

Juliet O break, my heart. Poor bankrupt, break at once.
60   To prison, eyes, ne'er look on liberty.
        Vile earth to earth resign, end motion here,
        And thou and Romeo press on heavy bier.

Nurse O Tybalt, Tybalt, the best friend I had.
        O courteous Tybalt, honest gentleman!
65   That ever I should live to see thee dead!

Juliet What storm is this that blows so contrary?
        Is Romeo slaughtered and is Tybalt dead?
        My dearest cousin and my dearer lord?
        Then dreadful trumpet sound the general doom,
70   For who is living if those two are gone?

Nurse Tybalt is gone, and Romeo banished.
        Romeo that killed him, he is banished.

Juliet O God! Did Romeo's hand shed Tybalt's blood?

Nurse It did, it did, alas the day, it did.

75 **Juliet** O serpent heart, hid with a flowering face.
        Did ever dragon keep so fair a cave?
        Beautiful tyrant, fiend angelical,
        Dove-feathered raven, wolfish-ravening lamb!
        Despised substance of divinest show!
80   Just opposite to what thou justly seem'st!
        A damned saint, an honourable villain!
        O nature what hadst thou to do in hell
        When thou didst bower the spirit of a fiend
        In mortal paradise of such sweet flesh?
85   Was ever book containing such vile matter
        So fairly bound? O, that deceit should dwell
        In such a gorgeous palace.

Nurse I saw the wound; I saw it with my own eyes—God save me—here on his manly chest. A pitiful corpse, a bloody pitiful corpse, pale, pale as ashes, all covered with blood, all gory blood. I fainted at the sight.

Juliet Oh, break, my heart. My poor ruined heart, break instantly. To prison, my eyes, and never look upon liberty again. My earthly body will be surrendered to earth, and life will end here. And my body will share one heavy funeral bed with Romeo.

Nurse Oh Tybalt! Tybalt! The best friend I had. Oh courteous Tybalt! Honest gentleman! That I should ever live to see you dead!

Juliet What storm is this that blows us so much grief? Is Romeo killed and is Tybalt dead? My dearest cousin and my even dearer husband? Then let the dreadful trumpet signal the end of the world. Who is living if these two are dead?

Nurse Tybalt is gone, and Romeo is banished from Verona. Romeo, who killed Tybalt, is banished!

Juliet Oh God! Did Romeo kill Tybalt?

Nurse He did, he did! Alas the day, he did!

Juliet Oh, the snake's heart that's disguised by a lovely face! Did a dragon ever live in such a beautiful cave? Beautiful wickedness! Angelic devil! Dove-like raven! Wolf-like lamb! Hateful reality that looks divine! Just the opposite of what you seem to be! Oh, damned saint! Honorable villain! Oh Nature, what were you doing in hell when you placed the spirit of a devil in such a paradise of lovely human flesh? Was there ever a book that contained such evil words inside such a beautiful cover? Oh, that deceit should live in such a gorgeous palace!

Nurse   There's no trust,
No faith, no honesty in men. All perjured,
90   All forsworn, all naught, all dissemblers.
Ah, where's my man? Give me some aqua vitae.
These griefs, these woes, these sorrows make me old.
Shame come to Romeo.

Juliet   Blistered be thy tongue
95   For such a wish. He was not born to shame.
Upon his brow shame is ashamed to sit,
For 'tis a throne where honour may be crowned
Sole monarch of the universal earth.
O, what a beast was I to chide at him.

100 **Nurse** Will you speak well of him that killed your cousin?

Juliet Shall I speak ill of him that is my husband?
Ah, poor my lord, what tongue shall smooth thy name
When I thy three-hours wife have mangled it?
But wherefore, villain, didst thou kill my cousin?
105 That villain cousin would have killed my husband.
Back, foolish tears, back to your native spring,
Your tributary drops belong to woe
Which you mistaking offer up to joy.
My husband lives, that Tybalt would have slain,
110 And Tybalt's dead, that would have slain my husband.
All this is comfort. Wherefore weep I then?
Some word there was, worser than Tybalt's death,
That murdered me. I would forget it fain,
But O, it presses to my memory
115 Like damned guilty deeds to sinners' minds.
Tybalt is dead and Romeo – banished.
That 'banished', that one word 'banished',
Hath slain ten thousand Tybalts: Tybalt's death
Was woe enough, if it had ended there.
120 Or if sour woe delights in fellowship
And needly will be ranked with other griefs,
Why followed not, when she said 'Tybalt's dead',

Nurse There's no trust, no loyalty, no honesty in men. They're all liars, all deceitful, all worthless, all false. Ah, where's my man Peter? Give me a drink of brandy. These griefs, these cares, these sorrows make me old. Shame on Romeo!

Juliet May your tongue grow blisters on it for making such a wish. He wasn't born with shame in his nature. Shame is ashamed to show itself in his face. In him, honor reigns as the supreme king of all the earth. Oh, what a beast I was to criticize him!

Nurse Will you speak well of the man who killed your cousin?

Juliet Should I speak ill of the man who is my husband? Ah, my poor husband, who shall speak well of your name when I, your wife of three hours, have attacked it? But why, villain, did you kill my cousin? That villain cousin would have killed my husband. My foolish tears, go back into my eyes. These tears should be shed for sorrow, but I'm shedding them for joy. My husband lives, whom Tybalt would have killed. And Tybalt's dead, who would have killed my husband. This is comforting. But why, then, am I weeping? A word was mentioned that murdered me, a word worse than Tybalt's death. I wish I could forget it. But it stays in my memory like evil deeds stay on sinners' minds. Tybalt is dead and Romeo—banished. That "banished," that one word "banished," could have killed ten thousand Tybalts. Tybalt's death was sorrow enough if it had ended there. But if bitter sorrow wants company and must be accompanied by other griefs, then why didn't she follow the words "Tybalt's dead"

Thy father or thy mother, nay or both,
Which modern lamentation might have moved?
125 But with a rearward following Tybalt's death,
'Romeo is banished': to speak that word
Is father, mother, Tybalt, Romeo, Juliet,
All slain, all dead. Romeo is banished.
There is no end, no limit, measure, bound,
130 In that word's death. No words can that woe sound.
Where is my father and my mother, Nurse?

Nurse Weeping and wailing over Tybalt's corse.
Will you go to them? I will bring you thither.

Juliet Wash they his wounds with tears? Mine shall be spent
135 When theirs are dry, for Romeo's banishment.
Take up those cords. Poor ropes, you are beguiled,
Both you and I, for Romeo is exiled.
He made you for a highway to my bed,
But I, a maid, die maiden-widowed.
140 Come, cords, come, Nurse, I'll to my wedding bed,
And death, not Romeo take my maidenhead.

Nurse Hie to your chamber. I'll find Romeo
To comfort you. I wot well where he is.
Hark ye, your Romeo will be here at night.
145 I'll to him. He is hid at Lawrence' cell.

Juliet O find him, give this ring to my true knight
And bid him come to take his last farewell.

[*Exeunt*]

with the words "and your father," or "and your mother," or even both? That would have moved me to a normal amount of grief. But to follow "Tybalt's dead" with "Romeo is banished"! To speak that word is like saying father, mother, Tybalt, Romeo, Juliet, all are killed, all are dead. Romeo is banished! There is no end, no limit, no measurement, no boundary to the death that word brings. No words can describe the depth of that sorrow. Where are my father and my mother, Nurse?

Nurse Weeping and wailing over Tybalt's corpse. Do you want to go to them? I'll take you there!

Juliet Do they cry as if to wash his wounds with their tears? My tears shall begin when theirs are dry, for Romeo's banishment! Pick up the ladder. Poor ropes. You've been cheated—both you and I have—for Romeo is exiled. He made you as a way to come to my bed. But I, a virgin, will die a virgin widow. Come, ropes. Come, Nurse. I'll go to my wedding bed. And death, not Romeo, will take my virginity.

Nurse Go to your bedroom. I'll find Romeo to comfort you. I know where he is. Listen, your Romeo will be here tonight. I'll go to him. He's hiding at Friar Lawrence's cell.

Juliet Oh, find him! Give this ring to my true love, and tell him to come and take his last farewell.

[**Juliet** *and the* **Nurse** *exit*]

Act III

Scene III

Friar Lawrence's cell. Enter **Friar Lawrence**

Friar Lawrence   Romeo, come forth, come forth, thou fearful man.
Affliction is enamoured of thy parts
And thou art wedded to calamity.

[*Enter* **Romeo**]

5   **Romeo**   Father, what news? What is the Prince's doom?
What sorrow craves acquaintance at my hand
That I yet know not?

Friar Lawrence   Too familiar
Is my dear son with such sour company.
10   I bring thee tidings of the Prince's doom.

Romeo   What less than doomsday is the Prince's doom?

Friar Lawrence   A gentler judgement vanished from his lips:
Not body's death but body's banishment.

Romeo   Ha! Banishment! Be merciful, say 'death'.
15   For exile hath more terror in his look,
Much more than death. Do not say 'banishment'.

Friar Lawrence   Hence from Verona art thou banished.
Be patient, for the world is broad and wide.

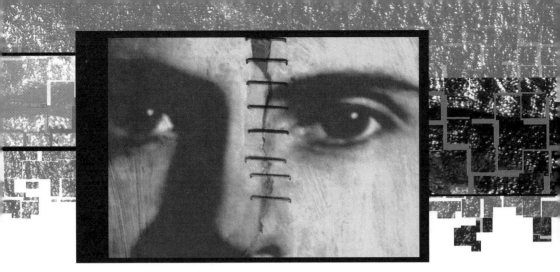

Friar Lawrence's chamber. **Friar Lawrence** *enters.*

Friar Lawrence   Romeo, come out, come out, you frightened man! Misfortune has learned to love you, and you're married to bad luck.

[**Romeo** *enters*]

Romeo   Father, what news? What's the Prince's judgment? What sorrow that I haven't met still wants to make my acquaintance?

Friar Lawrence   My dear son, you're too familiar with such bitter companions. I bring news of the Prince's penalty.

Romeo   What, short of doomsday, is the Prince's sentence?

Friar Lawrence   A judgment more gentle than death passed his lips: not death, but banishment.

Romeo   What! Banishment! Have mercy and say "death"! Exile is more terrifying, much more than death. Don't say "banishment."

Friar Lawrence   You're banished from Verona. But be patient. The world is broad and wide.

Romeo   There is no world without Verona walls
20   But purgatory, torture, hell itself;
        Hence 'banished' is banished from the world,
        And world's exile is death. Then 'banished'
        Is death, mistermed. Calling death 'banished'
        Thou cut'st my head off with a golden axe
25   And smilest upon the stroke that murders me.

Friar Lawrence   O deadly sin, O rude unthankfulness.
        Thy fault our law calls death, but the kind Prince,
        Taking thy part hath rushed aside the law
        And turned that black word 'death' to banishment.
30   This is dear mercy and thou seest it not.

Romeo   'Tis torture and not mercy. Heaven is here
        Where Juliet lives, and every cat and dog
        And little mouse, every unworthy thing,
        Live here in heaven and may look on her,
35   But Romeo may not. More validity,
        More honourable state, more courtship lives
        In carrion flies than Romeo. They may seize
        On the white wonder of dear Juliet's hand
        And steal immortal blessing from her lips,
40   Who, even in pure and vestal modesty
        Still blush, as thinking their won kisses sin.
        But Romeo may not, he is banished.
        Flies may do this, but I from this must fly.
        They are free men but I am banished.
45   And say'st thou yet that exile is not death?
        Hadst thou no poison mixed, no sharp-ground knife,
        No sudden mean of death, though ne'er so mean,
        But 'banished' to kill me? 'Banished'?
        O Friar, the damned use that word in hell.
50   Howling attends it. How hast thou the heart,
        Being a divine, a ghostly confessor,
        A sin-absolver, and my friend professed,
        To mangle me with that word 'banished'?

Romeo There's no world outside of Verona's walls except purgatory, torture, hell itself. Therefore, "banished" means banished from the world. And exile from the world means death. So "banished" is death, misnamed. When you call death "banished," you cut off my head with a golden axe and smile at the stroke that murders me.

Friar Lawrence What a deadly sin—oh, what rude ungratefulness! Under our law, your crime calls for the death penalty. But the kind Prince, being considerate to you, has thrust aside the law and turned that black word "death" to banishment. This is rare mercy, and you don't see it.

Romeo It's torture, not mercy. Heaven is here where Juliet lives. Every cat and dog and little mouse, every unworthy thing, lives here in heaven and can look at her. But Romeo can't. More value, more honorable status, more courtliness live in common flies than in Romeo. They may land upon the white wonder of dear Juliet's hand and steal a heavenly kiss from her lips—those lips that still blush with pure and virginal modesty, thinking that they sin when they touch each other. But Romeo can't. He's banished. Flies may do this, but I must fly from here. They're free, but I'm banished. And you still say that exile isn't death? Don't you have poison, or a sharp-edged knife, or some other quick means of death, no matter now dishonorable—other than "banished"—to execute me? "Banished"! Oh Friar! The souls of the damned use that word in hell. That word goes with howling. How can you have the heart to tear me apart with that word "banished"—being a priest, a spiritual confessor, a forgiver of sins, and calling yourself my friend?

Friar Lawrence Thou fond mad man, hear me a little speak.

55 **Romeo** O, thou wilt speak again of banishment.

Friar Lawrence I'll give thee armour to keep off that word,
  Adversity's sweet milk, philosophy,
  To comfort thee though thou art banished.

Romeo Yet 'banished'? Hang up philosophy.
60 Unless philosophy can make a Juliet,
  Displant a town, reverse a Prince's doom,
  It helps not, it prevails not. Talk no more.

Friar Lawrence O, then I see that mad men have no ears.

Romeo How should they when that wise men have no eyes?

65 **Friar Lawrence** Let me dispute with thee of thy estate.

Romeo Thou canst not speak of that thou dost not feel.
  Wert thou as young as I, Juliet thy love,
  An hour but married, Tybalt murdered,
  Doting like me, and like me banished,
70 Then mightst thou speak, then mightst thou tear thy hair
  And fall upon the ground as I do now,
  Taking the measure of an unmade grave.

  [*Knock*]

Friar Lawrence Arise, one knocks. Good Romeo, hide
  thyself.

75 **Romeo** Not I, unless the breath of heartsick groans
  Mist-like infold me from the search of eyes.

  [*Knock*]

Friar Lawrence Hark how they knock! Who's there? Romeo,
  arise,
  Thou wilt be taken! Stay awhile! Stand up!

Friar Lawrence   You foolish, irrational man! Listen to me for a minute.

Romeo   Oh, you'll just talk more about banishment.

Friar Lawrence   I'll give you some protection against that word. You can be consoled in misfortune by keeping a philosophical frame of mind. That will give you comfort, even though you're banished.

Romeo   Still talking "banished"? Hang philosophy! Unless philosophy can make a Juliet, move a town, and reverse a Prince's sentence, it doesn't help. It has no effect. Say no more.

Friar Lawrence   Oh, then I see that madmen have no ears!

Romeo   Why should they, when wise men have no eyes?

Friar Lawrence   Let's talk about your situation.

Romeo   You can't talk about something you don't feel. If you were as young as I am, with Juliet as your love, and married just an hour, with Tybalt murdered; and if you were madly in love like me, and like me banished, then you could speak! Then you might tear out your hair and throw yourself on the ground, as I do now, taking the measurement for my unmade grave.

[*A knock is heard at the door*]

Friar Lawrence   Get up, someone's knocking. Good Romeo, hide yourself!

Romeo   No, I won't, unless the mist from my heartsick groans hides me!

[*The knocking continues*]

Friar Lawrence   Listen, they're knocking! Who's there? Romeo, get up! You'll be captured! Wait a minute! Stand up!

[*Knock*]

80   Run to my study! By and by! God's will,
What simpleness is this? I come, I come!

[*Knock*]

Who knocks so hard? Whence come you, what's your will?

Nurse [*Within*] Let me come in and you shall know my
errand. I come from Lady Juliet.

85 **Friar Lawrence**   Welcome then.

[*Enter* **Nurse**]

Nurse O holy Friar, tell me, holy Friar,
Where is my lady's lord, where's Romeo?

Friar Lawrence There on the ground, with his own tears
made drunk.

90 **Nurse** O, he is even in my mistress' case.
Just in her case. O woeful sympathy,
Piteous predicament. Even so lies she,
Blubbering and weeping, weeping and blubbering.
Stand up, stand up! Stand, and you be a man!
95 For Juliet's sake, for her sake, rise and stand!
Why should you fall into so deep an O?

[*He rises*]

Romeo Nurse.

Nurse   Ah sir, ah sir, death's the end of all.

[*More knocking*]

Run to my study! In a minute! God's will! What stupidity is this? I'm coming, I'm coming!

[*Knocking, louder now*]

Who's knocking so hard? Where do you come from? What do you want?

Nurse [*from offstage*] Let me come in, and I'll tell you what I want. I come from the Lady Juliet.

Friar Lawrence Welcome, then.

[*The* **Nurse** *enters*]

Nurse Oh holy Friar! Oh, tell me, holy Friar, where's my lady's husband? Where's Romeo?

Friar Lawrence There on the ground, drunk with his own tears.

Nurse Oh, he's in the same condition as my mistress. Just the same! Oh, how alike in their suffering. What a pitiful predicament. She's just like that—sobbing and weeping, weeping and sobbing. Stand up! Stand up! Stand, and be a man! For Juliet's sake, for her sake, rise and stand! Why should you fall into such a deep fit of groaning?

[**Romeo** *rises*]

Romeo Nurse!

Nurse Ah, sir! Ah, sir! Death is the end of all of us.

Romeo   Spak'st thou of Juliet? How is it with her?
100   Doth not she think me an old murderer
Now I have stained the childhood of our joy
With blood removed but little from her own?
Where is she? And how doth she? And what says
My concealed lady to our cancelled love?

105 **Nurse**   O she says nothing, sir, but weeps and weeps,
And now falls on her bed, and then starts up,
And Tybalt calls, and then on Romeo cries,
And then down falls again.

Romeo   As if that name,
110   Shot from the deadly level of a gun,
Did murder her, as that name's cursed hand
Murdered her kinsman. O, tell me, Friar, tell me,
In what vile part of this anatomy
Doth my name lodge? Tell me that I may sack
115   The hateful mansion!

Friar Lawrence   Hold thy desperate hand.
Art thou a man? Thy form cries out thou art.
Thy tears are womanish, thy wild acts denote
The unreasonable fury of a beast.
120   Unseemly woman in a seeming man,
And ill-beseeming beast in seeming both!
Thou hast amazed me. By my holy order,
I thought thy disposition better tempered.
Hast thou slain Tybalt? Wilt thou slay thyself?
125   And slay thy lady that in thy life lives,
By doing damned hate upon thyself?
Why rail'st thou on thy birth, the heaven and earth?
Since birth, and heaven, and earth all three do meet
In thee at once; which thou at once would lose.
130   Fie, fie, thou sham'st thy shape, thy love, thy wit,
Which, like a usurer, abound'st in all,
And usest none in that true use indeed
Which should bedeck thy shape, thy love, thy wit.

Romeo Did you speak of Juliet? How is she? Does she think I'm an old murderer, now that I've ruined the newness of our joy with the blood of a close relative? Where is she? And how is she? And what does my secret bride say about our cancelled love?

Nurse Oh, she says nothing sir, but weeps and weeps. She falls on her bed, and then she gets up, and calls out "Tybalt," and then cries out "Romeo," and she falls down again.

Romeo It's as if my name had murdered her, shot with a deadly aim from a gun, just as that name's cursed hand murdered her cousin! Oh, tell me, Friar, tell me. In what vile part of my body does my name live? Tell me so I can attack the hated place!

[*He draws his dagger to stab himself, but the* **Nurse** *snatches it away*]

Friar Lawrence Stop your desperate act! Are you a man? You look like one, but your tears are womanish, and your wild behavior seems like the thoughtless fury of a beast. You seem like a man, but act like an unseemly, improper woman. Seeming to be both a man and a woman makes you an ugly beast! You amaze me. By my holy vow, I thought you had a more composed character. So you've killed Tybalt? Will you kill yourself? And kill your wife, who's one with your life, damning yourself with suicide? Why do you rave on about your birth, the soul, and the body? Since birth, soul, and body all three are combined in you, and you would immediately lose all three. Shame! Shame! You disgrace your human body, your love, your intelligence! Like a moneylender, you have many possessions, but you don't use them for their proper purpose, which is to improve your body, your love, and your intelligence.

Thy noble shape is but a form of wax
135 Digressing from the valour of a man;
Thy dear love sworn but hollow perjury,
Killing that love which thou hast vowed to cherish;
Thy wit, that ornament to shape and love,
Misshapen in the conduct of them both,
140 Like powder in a skilless soldier's flask
Is set afire by thine own ignorance,
And thou dismembered with thine own defence.
What, rouse thee, man! Thy Juliet is alive,
For whose dear sake thou wast but lately dead.
145 There art thou happy. Tybalt would kill thee,
But thou slew'st Tybalt. There art thou happy.
The law that threatened death becomes thy friend
And turns it to exile. There art thou happy.
A pack of blessings light upon thy back;
150 Happiness courts thee in her best array;
But like a misbehaved and sullen wench
Thou pouts upon thy fortune and thy love.
Take heed, take heed, for such die miserable.
Go, get thee to thy love, as was decreed,
155 Ascend her chamber; hence, and comfort her.
But look thou stay not till the watch be set,
For then thou can'st not pass to Mantua,
Where thou shalt live till we can find a time
To blaze your marriage, reconcile your friends,
160 Beg pardon of the Prince, and call thee back
With twenty hundred thousand times more joy
Than thou went'st forth in lamentation.
Go before, Nurse. Commend me to thy lady,
And bid her hasten all the house to bed,
165 Which heavy sorrow makes them apt unto.
Romeo is coming.

Nurse   O Lord, I could have stayed here all the night
To hear good counsel. O what learning is!
My lord, I'll tell my lady you will come.

Your noble body is like a figure of wax, lacking the courage of a man. The love that you swore was a lie, killing the love you vowed to cherish. That ornament of the body and of love, your intelligence, is mistaken in the guidance it gives them both. You're blown apart by what should be your defense, the way gunpowder gets ignited in an inexperienced soldier's powder horn. Here! Stir yourself, man! Your Juliet is alive, for whose dear sake you just now wished to be dead. You're fortunate in that! Tybalt would have killed you, but you killed Tybalt. You're fortunate in that! The law that threatened you with death becomes your friend, and turns your penalty into exile. You're fortunate in that! You've had many blessings fall on you. Happiness comes to court you in her best attire. But like a misbehaved and sullen girl, you pout about your fortune and your love. Be careful, be careful: People like that die miserable. Go on; go see your love as you planned. Climb into her room. Go on, comfort her. But watch that you don't stay until the night guards are posted. Then you couldn't leave for Mantua, where you'll live until we find the right time to announce your marriage, reconcile your relatives, beg the Prince's pardon, and call you back with twenty hundred thousand times more joy than when you left in sorrow. Go ahead, Nurse. My greetings to your lady. Tell her to urge everyone to go to bed early, which their heavy sorrow makes them ready to do. Romeo is coming.

Nurse Oh Lord, I could've stayed here all night to hear your good advice. Oh, what education is! [*To* **Romeo**] My lord, I'll tell my lady you're coming.

170 **Romeo** Do so, and bid my sweet prepare to chide.

Nurse Here, sir, a ring she bid me give you, sir.
Hie you, make haste, for it grows very late.

[*Exit* **Nurse**]

Romeo How well my comfort is revived by this.

Friar Lawrence Go hence, good night, and here stands all
175   your state:
Either be gone before the Watch be set,
Or by the break of day disguised from hence.
Sojourn in Mantua. I'll find out your man,
And he shall signify from time to time
180   Every good hap to you that chances here.
Give me thy hand. 'Tis late. Farewell. Good night.

Romeo But that a joy past joy calls out on me,
It were a grief so brief to part with thee.
Farewell.

[*Exeunt*]

Romeo Do so, and tell my sweet one to be ready to scold me.

Nurse Here, sir, is a ring that she told me to give you, sir.
Hurry. Make haste, for it's getting very late.

[*The* **Nurse** *exits*]

Romeo How well my spirits are revived by this!

Friar Lawrence Go on. Good night! Your situation depends
on this: Either be gone before the guard is posted, or leave
here in disguise by daybreak. Stay in Mantua. I'll find your
servant, and he'll get you messages from time to time about
every piece of good news that happens here. Give me your
hand. It's late. Farewell. Good night.

Romeo If it weren't for a great joy—greater than joy itself—
that calls me away, it would be sad to part from you in such
a hurry. Farewell.

[**Romeo** *and* **Friar Lawrence** *exit*]

Act III

Scene IV

Capulet's house. Enter **Capulet, Lady Capulet** *and* **Paris**

Capulet   Things have fallen out, sir, so unluckily
That we have had no time to move our daughter.
Look you, she loved her kinsman Tybalt dearly,
And so did I. Well, we were born to die.
5   'Tis very late. She'll not come down tonight.
I promise you, but for your company,
I would have been abed an hour ago.

Paris   These times of woe afford no times to woo.
Madam, good night. Commend me to your daughter.

10   **Lady Capulet**   I will, and know her mind early tomorrow.
Tonight she's mewed up to her heaviness.

[**Paris** *offers to go in and* **Capulet** *calls him again*]

Capulet   Sir Paris, I will make a desperate tender
Of my child's love. I think she will be ruled
In all respects by me; nay, more, I doubt it not.
15   Wife, go you to her ere you go to bed,
Acquaint her here of my son Paris' love,
And bid her – mark you me? – on Wednesday next –
But soft – what day is this?

Paris   Monday, my lord.

Capulet's house. **Capulet, Lady Capulet,** *and* **Paris** *enter.*

Capulet Such unlucky things have happened, sir, and we haven't had time to talk to our daughter about you. You see, she loved her cousin Tybalt dearly, and so did I. Well, we were born to die! It's very late. She won't come down tonight, I assure you. Except for your company, I would have been in bed an hour ago.

Paris These times of grief are not times for courtship. Madam, good night. Give my regards to your daughter.

Lady Capulet I will, and I'll know what she thinks by early tomorrow. Tonight she's shut up with her sorrow.

[**Paris** *starts to leave, but* **Capulet** *calls him back again*]

Capulet Sir Paris. I'll make a bold offer of my child's love. I think she'll be ruled by me in all respects. No, even more— I don't doubt it. Wife, go to her before you go to bed. Tell her about my son-in-law Paris's love. Tell her—do you understand?—that Wednesday— But wait—what day is it today?

Paris Monday, my lord.

20 **Capulet** Monday! Ha ha! Well, Wednesday is too soon.
A Thursday let it be, a Thursday, tell her,
She shall be married to this noble earl.
Will you be ready? Do you like this haste?
We'll keep no great ado – a friend or two.
25 For, hark you, Tybalt being slain so late,
It may be thought we held him carelessly,
Being our kinsman, if we revel much.
Therefore we'll have some half a dozen friends
And there an end. But what say you to Thursday?

30 **Paris** My lord, I would that Thursday were tomorrow.

Capulet Well, get you gone. A Thursday be it then.
Go you to Juliet ere you go to bed,
Prepare her, wife, against this wedding day.
Farewell, my lord. Light to my chamber, ho!
35 Afore me, it is so very late that we
May call it early by and by. Good night.

[Exeunt]

Capulet Monday! Ah. . . . Well, Wednesday is too soon. Let it be on Thursday. Thursday, tell her, she'll be married to this noble earl. Will you be ready? Do you approve of this haste? We won't have a big affair—just a friend or two. Because, with our relative Tybalt being killed so recently, people might think that we don't hold him in high regard if we have a large party. So we'll have just a half-dozen friends, and that's all. What do you say to Thursday?

Paris My lord, I wish that Thursday were tomorrow!

Capulet Well, be off with you. On Thursday it will be, then. [*To* **Lady Capulet**] Go to Juliet before you go to bed. Prepare her, wife, for this wedding day. [*To* **Paris**] Farewell, my lord. [*To his* **Servant**] Bring lights to my bedroom, there! I say, it's so very late that we may soon be calling it early. Good night.

[*They exit*]

Act III

Scene V

Juliet's bedroom. **Romeo** *and* **Juliet** *stand at the window*

Juliet Wilt thou be gone? It is not yet near day.
It was the nightingale and not the lark
That pierced the fearful hollow of thine ear.
Nightly she sings on yond pomegranate tree.
5   Believe me, love, it was the nightingale.

Romeo It was the lark, the herald of the morn,
No nightingale. Look, love, what envious streaks
Do lace the severing clouds in yonder east.
Night's candles are burnt out, and jocund day
10   Stands tiptoe on the misty mountain tops.
I must be gone and live, or stay and die.

Juliet Yond light is not daylight, I know it, I.
It is some meteor that the sun exhales
To be to thee this night a torchbearer
15   And light thee on thy way to Mantua.
Therefore stay yet: thou need'st not to be gone.

Romeo Let me be ta'en, let me be put to death.
I am content, so thou wilt have it so.
I'll say yon grey is not the morning's eye,
20   'Tis but the pale reflex of Cynthia's brow.
Nor that is not the lark whose notes do beat
The vaulty heaven so high above our heads.
I have more care to stay than will to go.
Come death, and welcome. Juliet wills it so.
25   How is't, my soul? Let's talk. It is not day.

Juliet's bedroom. **Romeo** *and* **Juliet** *stand at the window.*

Juliet   Do you have to go? It's not yet near daylight. It was the nightingale and not the lark that you heard and that caused you to worry. Every night she sings on that pomegranate tree over there. Believe me, love, it was the nightingale.

Romeo   It was the lark, who signals the morning, not the nightingale. Look, my love, at the envious streaks of daylight piercing the clouds in the east. The stars, night's candles, have faded. Beautiful day stands on tip-toe on the misty mountaintops. I must be gone and live, or stay and die.

Juliet   That light is not daylight. I know it. It's a meteor from the sun, which will be a torchbearer tonight to light you on your way to Mantua. So stay a little while. You don't have to leave.

Romeo   Let me be captured. Let me be put to death. I'm happy if that's what you wish. I'll say that gray light is not morning light—it's just a pale reflection of the moon. And that's not the lark whose song rises to heaven, far above us. I have more desire to stay than will to go. Come, death, and welcome. Juliet wishes it so. How are you, my love? Let's talk. It is not day.

Juliet   It is, it is. Hie hence, begone, away.
    It is the lark that sings so out of tune,
    Straining harsh discords and unpleasing sharps.
    Some say the lark makes sweet division.
30   This doth not so, for she divideth us.
    Some say the lark and loathed toad change eyes.
    O, now I would they had changed voices too,
    Since arm from arm that voice doth us affray,
    Hunting thee hence with hunt's-up to the day.
35   O now be gone, more light and light it grows.

Romeo   More light and light: more dark and dark our woes.

[*Enter* **Nurse** *hastily*]

Nurse   Madam.

Juliet   Nurse?

Nurse   Your lady mother is coming to your chamber.
40   The day is broke, be wary, look about.

[*Exit*]

Juliet   Then, window, let day in and let life out.

Romeo   Farewell, farewell. One kiss and I'll descend.

[*He goes down*]

Juliet   Art thou gone so? Love, lord, ay husband, friend,
    I must hear from thee every day in the hour,
45   For in a minute there are many days.
    O, by this count I shall be much in years
    Ere I again behold my Romeo.

Romeo   Farewell.
    I will omit no opportunity
50   That may convey my greetings, love, to thee.

Juliet It is! It is! Leave now. Be gone. Go away! It is the lark that sings so out of tune, with its harsh and shrill sounds. Some say the lark makes sweet musical chords. This lark does not, for she causes us to separate. Some say the lark and the hideous toad exchanged eyes. Now I wish they had exchanged voices, too, since we are torn from each other's arms by the lark's voice, which chases you away, as the morning call wakes the huntsman. Leave now. It is growing lighter.

Romeo The lighter it grows, the darker our woes.

[*The* **Nurse** *enters in haste*]

Nurse Madam!

Juliet Nurse?

Nurse Your mother is coming to your bedroom. It's daybreak. Be careful! Watch out!

[*The* **Nurse** *exits*]

Juliet Well then, window, let the day in and let life out.

Romeo Good-bye. Good-bye. One kiss and I'll climb down.

[*He climbs down*]

Juliet Are you gone? Love, lord, yes husband, friend. I must hear from you every hour of the day, because in each minute there are many days. Oh, by this count I'll be old before I see my Romeo again.

Romeo Good-bye. I won't miss any chance to send word to you, my love.

Juliet O think'st thou we shall ever meet again?

Romeo I doubt it not, and all these woes shall serve
For sweet discourses in our times to come.

Juliet O God, I have an ill-divining soul!
55 Methinks I see thee, now thou art so low,
As one dead in the bottom of a tomb.
Either my eyesight fails, or thou look'st pale.

Romeo And trust me, love, in my eye so do you.
Dry sorrow drinks our blood. Adieu, adieu.

[*Exit*]

60 **Juliet** O Fortune, Fortune! All men call thee fickle;
If thou art fickle, what dost thou with him
That is renowned for faith? Be fickle, Fortune,
For then I hope thou wilt not keep him long,
But send him back.

[*Enter* **Lady Capulet**]

65 **Lady Capulet** Ho, daughter, are you up?

Juliet Who is't that calls? It is my lady mother.
Is she not down so late, or up so early?
What unaccustomed cause procures her hither?

[*She goes down from the window*]

Lady Capulet Why, how now Juliet?

70 **Juliet** Madam, I am not well.

Lady Capulet Evermore weeping for your cousin's death?
What, wilt thou wash him from his grave with tears?
And if thou couldst, thou couldst not make him live.
Therefore have done. Some grief shows much of love,
75 But much of grief shows still some want of wit.

Juliet Oh, do you think we'll ever meet again?

Romeo I don't doubt it. We'll talk and laugh about all these sorrows in times to come.

Juliet Oh God! I have a feeling some evil is coming. I think I see you—now you're down so low—as if you're a dead person at the bottom of a tomb. Either my eyesight is failing, or you look pale.

Romeo Trust me, my love, so do you. Thirsty sorrow drains our blood. Farewell! Farewell!

[**Romeo** *exits*]

Juliet Oh Fortune, Fortune! Everyone calls you fickle. If you are fickle, what business do you have with Romeo, who's well-known for faithfulness? Be fickle, Fortune, because then I hope you won't keep him long, but send him back to me.

[**Lady Capulet** *enters*]

Lady Capulet Daughter! Are you up?

Juliet Who's calling? It's my mother. Hasn't she gone to bed yet, or is she up early? What could have happened to bring her here?

[**Juliet** *steps down from the window*]

Lady Capulet Why, what's wrong, Juliet?

Juliet Madam, I'm not well.

Lady Capulet Are you still weeping for your cousin's death? What, will you wash him out of his grave with tears? Even if you could, you couldn't make him live again. So stop crying. Some expression of grief shows love. Too much grief is foolishness.

Juliet Yet let me weep for such a feeling loss.

Lady Capulet So shall you feel the loss but not the friend
Which you weep for.

Juliet   Feeling so the loss,
80   I cannot choose but ever weep the friend.

Lady Capulet Well, girl, thou weepst not so much for his death
As that the villain lives which slaughtered him.

Juliet What villain, madam?

85 **Lady Capulet**   That same villain Romeo.

Juliet Villain and he be many miles asunder.
God pardon him. I do with all my heart.
And yet no man like he doth grieve my heart.

Lady Capulet That is because the traitor murderer lives.

90 **Juliet** Ay madam, from the reach of these my hands.
Would none but I might venge my cousin's death.

Lady Capulet We will have vengeance for it, fear thou not.
Then weep no more. I'll send to one in Mantua,
Where that same banished runagate doth live,
95   Shall give him such an unaccustomed dram
That he shall soon keep Tybalt company;
And then I hope thou wilt be satisfied.

Juliet Indeed I never shall be satisfied
With Romeo, till I behold him – dead –
100   Is my poor heart so for a kinsman vexed.
Madam, if you could find out but a man
To bear a poison, I would temper it –
That Romeo should upon receipt thereof
Soon sleep in quiet. O, how my heart abhors
105   To hear him named, and cannot come to him
To wreak the love I bore my cousin
Upon his body that hath slaughtered him.

Juliet Let me weep for such a terrible loss.

Lady Capulet You'll feel the loss, but the friend that you're weeping for cannot feel.

Juliet I feel the loss so much that I can't help but continue weeping for the friend.

Lady Capulet Well, girl, you're not weeping so much for his death, as because the villain who killed him is still alive.

Juliet What villain, madam?

Lady Capulet That villain Romeo.

Juliet [*to herself*] He's miles from being a villain. [*To* **Lady Capulet**] God forgive him! I do, with all my heart. And yet no man grieves my heart as much as he does.

Lady Capulet That is because the traitorous murderer lives.

Juliet Yes, madam—beyond the reach of my hands. I wish that I alone might avenge my cousin's death!

Lady Capulet We'll have vengeance for it, don't worry. So don't weep any more. I'll send someone to Mantua, where that banished fugitive lives. He'll give him such a strange drink that he'll soon keep Tybalt company. And then I hope you'll be satisfied.

Juliet Indeed, I'll never be satisfied with Romeo until I see him—dead [*she continues with a new thought to avoid saying she wants Romeo dead*] is my poor heart, which mourns so for my kinsman. Madam, if you could find the man to carry the poison, I would mix it, so that Romeo, on receiving it, would soon sleep quietly. Oh, how my heart hates to hear his name, when I can't go to repay the love I had for my cousin upon the body that killed him.

Lady Capulet Find thou the means and I'll find such a man.
    But now I'll tell thee joyful tidings, girl.

110 **Juliet** And joy comes well in such a needy time.
    What are they, I beseech your ladyship?

Lady Capulet Well, well, thou hast a careful father, child;
    One who to put thee from thy heaviness
    Hath sorted out a sudden day of joy,
115   That thou expects not, nor I looked not for.

Juliet Madam, in happy time. What day is that?

Lady Capulet Marry, my child, early next Thursday morn
    The gallant, young, and noble gentleman,
    The County Paris, at Saint Peter's Church,
120   Shall happily make thee there a joyful bride.

Juliet Now by Saint Peter's Church, and Peter too,
    He shall not make me there a joyful bride.
    I wonder at this haste, that I must wed
    Ere he that should be husband comes to woo.
125   I pray you tell my lord and father, madam,
    I will not marry yet. And when I do, I swear
    It shall be Romeo, whom you know I hate,
    Rather than Paris. These are news indeed.

Lady Capulet Here comes your father, tell him so yourself,
130   And see how he will take it at your hands.

[*Enter* **Capulet** *and* **Nurse**]

Capulet When the sun sets the earth doth drizzle dew,
    But for the sunset of my brother's son
    It rains downright.
    How now, a conduit, girl? What, still in tears?
135   Evermore showering? In one little body
    Thou counterfeits a bark, a sea, a wind.
    For still thy eyes, which I may call the sea,

Lady Capulet [*Taking "repay" to mean "avenge"*] You find the means and I'll find the man. But now, I'll tell you some good news, girl.

Juliet Good news is welcome at such a needy time. What is it, may I ask your ladyship?

Lady Capulet Well, well, you have a father who is concerned for your welfare, child. To raise your sad spirits he has arranged a day of joy for you that soon will be here. It's something you have not expected, nor have I.

Juliet Madam, a timely joy. What day is that?

Lady Capulet Well, my child, early this Thursday morning the gallant, young, and noble gentleman, Count Paris, will happily make you a joyful bride at Saint Peter's Church!

Juliet Now by Saint Peter's Church and Peter too, he won't make me a joyful bride there! I'm astonished at this haste, that I must marry before the one who's to be my husband comes to court me! Please, madam, tell my lord and father that I will not marry yet. And when I do, I swear it shall be Romeo—whom you know I hate—rather than Paris. This is news indeed!

Lady Capulet Here comes your father. Tell him so yourself, and see how he takes it from you.

[**Capulet** *and the* **Nurse** *enter*]

Capulet When the sun sets, the dew falls. But with the sunset of my brother's son, it downright rains! What's this, girl— are you a fountain? What, still crying? A continuous shower? In one little body you imitate a boat, a sea, a wind. Your eyes, which I'll call the sea, ebb and flow with tears. Your body is

Do ebb and flow with tears. The bark thy body is,
Sailing in this salt flood, the winds thy sighs,
140 Who raging with thy tears and they with them,
Without a sudden calm will overset
Thy tempest-tossed body. How now, wife?
Have you delivered to her our decree?

Lady Capulet Ay sir, but she will none, she gives you thanks.
145 I would the fool were married to her grave.

Capulet Soft. Take me with you, take me with you, wife.
How? Will she none? Doth she not give us thanks?
Is she not proud? Doth she not count her blest,
Unworthy as she is, that we have wrought
150 So worthy a gentleman to be her bride?

Juliet Not proud you have, but thankful that you have.
Proud can I never be of what I hate,
But thankful even for hate that is meant love.

Capulet How, how, how, how? Chopped logic? What is this?
155 'Proud' and 'I thank you' and 'I thank you not'
And yet 'not proud'? Mistress minion you,
Thank me no thankings nor proud me no prouds,
But fettle your fine joints 'gainst Thursday next
To go with Paris to Saint Peter's Church,
160 Or I will drag thee on a hurdle thither.
Out, you green-sickness carrion! Out, you baggage!
You tallow-face!

Lady Capulet Fie, fie. What, are you mad?

Juliet Good father, I beseech you on my knees.
165 Hear me with patience but to speak a word.

the boat, sailing in this salt ocean. Your sighs are the winds—
which, raging against the tears while your tears rage against
the sighs, will overturn your storm-tossed body unless
there's a sudden calm. How are you, wife? Have you told her
about our decision?

Lady Capulet Yes, sir. She says thank you but she'll have none
of it. I wish the fool were married to her grave!

Capulet Wait! I don't follow you! I don't follow you, wife! What
do you mean, she'll have none of it? Isn't she grateful to us?
Isn't she proud? Unworthy as she is, doesn't she think she's
blessed with luck that we've found such a worthy gentleman
to be her bridegroom?

Juliet I'm not proud that you have, but I'm grateful that you
have. I can never be proud about what I hate, but I can be
grateful, since what I hate is what you meant for me to love.

Capulet What are you saying? What are you saying?
Nitpicking? What is this—"proud" and "I'm grateful," and
"no thanks," and even "not proud." You spoiled child! Thank
me no thankings and proud me no prouds! Just prepare
your fine self to go with Paris to Saint Peter's Church next
Thursday, or I'll drag you there in a cart. How dare you! You
anemic thing! How dare you! You good-for-nothing! You
coward!

Lady Capulet Shame on you! Shame on you! Are you mad?

Juliet Good father, I beg you on my knees. Be patient and
listen to just one word I have to say—

Capulet   Hang thee young baggage, disobedient wretch!
I tell thee what – get thee to church a Thursday
Or never after look me in the face.
Speak not, reply not, do not answer me.
170   My fingers itch. Wife, we scarce thought us blest
That God had lent us but this only child;
But now I see this one is one too much,
And that we have a curse in having her.
Out on her, hilding.

175   **Nurse**   God in heaven bless her.
You are to blame, my lord, to rate her so.

Capulet   And why, my Lady Wisdom? Hold your tongue,
Good Prudence! Smatter with your gossips, go.

Nurse   I speak no treason.

180   **Capulet**   O God 'i' good e'en!

Nurse   May not one speak?

Capulet   Peace, you mumbling fool!
Utter your gravity o'er a gossip's bowl,
For here we need it not.

185   **Lady Capulet**   You are too hot.

Capulet   God's bread, it makes me mad! Day, night, work,
      play,
Alone, in company, still my care hath been
To have her matched. And having now provided
190   A gentleman of noble parentage,
Of fair demesnes, youthful and nobly ligned,
Stuffed, as they say, with honourable parts,
Proportioned as one's thought would wish a man –
And then to have a wretched puling fool,
195   A whining mammet, in her fortune's tender,
To answer 'I'll not wed, I cannot love,
I am too young, I pray you pardon me!'
But, and you will not wed, I'll pardon you!

Capulet Hang you, you good-for-nothing, disobedient creature! I'll tell you what—get yourself to church on Thursday or never look me in the face again. Shut up! Don't answer me back! My fingers are itching! Wife, we thought we were blessed that God gave us this only child. But now I see that this is one too many, and we're cursed in having her. How dare she! Worthless creature!

Nurse God in heaven bless her. You're to blame, my lord, to yell at her like that.

Capulet And why, my Lady Wisdom? Hold your tongue, Madam Know-It-All! Go chatter with your gossipy friends!

Nurse I didn't say anything disloyal—

Capulet For God's sake, go on with you!

Nurse Can't a person speak?

Capulet Be quiet, you mumbling fool! Save your wisdom for your gossip's circle! We don't need it here!

Lady Capulet You're too excited!

Capulet By God's bread, it makes me mad! Day and night, at work, at play, alone, in company—all I think about is how to get her a husband. And now I've found a gentleman from a noble family, with beautiful estates, youthful, well-connected —a man who's stuffed, as they say, with honorable qualities. As handsome a man as one could wish. And then to have a wretched whimpering fool, a whining doll, when good fortune's offered to her, answer, "I won't marry! I cannot love, I'm too young, please pardon me!" [*Turning to* **Juliet**] But if you don't marry, I'll "pardon" you! Go feed

Graze where you will, you shall not house with me.
200 Look to't, think on't, I do not use to jest.
Thursday is near. Lay hand on heart. Advise.
And you be mine I'll give you to my friend;
And you be not, hang! Beg! Starve! Die in the streets!
For by my soul I'll ne'er acknowledge thee,
205 Nor what is mine shall never do thee good.
Trust to't, bethink you. I'll not be forsworn.

[*Exit*]

Juliet Is there no pity sitting in the clouds
That sees into the bottom of my grief?
O sweet my mother, cast me not away,
210 Delay this marriage for a month, a week,
Or if you do not, make the bridal bed
In that dim monument where Tybalt lies.

Lady Capulet Talk not to me, for I'll not speak a word.
Do as thou wilt, for I have done with thee.

[*Exit*]

215 **Juliet** O God, O Nurse, how shall this be prevented?
My husband is on earth, my faith in heaven.
How shall that faith return again to earth
Unless that husband send it me from heaven
By leaving earth? Comfort me, counsel me.
220 Alack, alack, that heaven should practise stratagems
Upon so soft a subject as myself.
What sayst thou? Hast thou not a word of joy?
Some comfort, Nurse.

Nurse   Faith, here it is.
225 Romeo is banished, and all the world to nothing
That he dares ne'er come back to challenge you.
Or if he do, it needs must be by stealth.
Then, since the case so stands as now it doth,

where you want to, you won't live in my house! See to it. Think about it. I'm not accustomed to joking. Thursday is near. Look into your heart. Consider it well. If you're my daughter, I'll give you to my friend. If you're not, you can go hang! Beg! Starve! Die in the streets! By my soul, I'll never acknowledge you as my daughter, and you'll never get anything from me. Believe it! So think about it! I won't go back on my word!

[**Capulet** *exits*]

Juliet Is there no pity in heaven that sees into the depths of my grief? Oh, sweet mother, don't cast me away. Delay this marriage for a month, a week, or if you don't, make the bridal bed in that dark tomb where Tybalt lies.

Lady Capulet Don't talk to me. I won't say a word. Do as you wish, I'm done with you.

[**Lady Capulet** *exits*]

Juliet Oh God! Oh Nurse! How can this be prevented? My husband is alive, my marriage vow is sworn in heaven. How can I marry again, unless my husband dies and sends my vow back to me from heaven? Comfort me. Advise me. Alas, alas, that heaven should play tricks upon so weak a person as myself. What do you say? Don't you have a cheerful word? Some comfort, Nurse?

Nurse By my faith, here it is: Romeo is banished, and you can bet the world that he'll never dare to come back to claim you. Or if he does, he'll have to do it in secret. So, the way

I think it best you married with the County.
230 O, he's a lovely gentleman.
Romeo's a dishclout to him. An eagle, madam,
Hath not so green, so quick, so fair an eye
As Paris hath. Beshrew my very heart,
I think you are happy in this second match,
235 For it excels your first; or, if it did not,
Your first is dead, or 'twere as good he were
As living here and you no use of him.

Juliet Speakest thou from thy heart?

Nurse And from my soul too, else beshrew them both.

240 **Juliet** Amen.

Nurse What?

Juliet Well, thou hast comforted me marvellous much.
Go in, and tell my lady I am gone,
Having displeased my father, to Lawrence' cell,
245 To make confession and to be absolved.

Nurse Marry, I will; and this is wisely done.

[*Exit*]

Juliet Ancient damnation! O most wicked fiend,
Is it more sin to wish me thus forsworn,
Or to dispraise my lord with that same tongue
250 Which she hath praised him with above compare
So many thousand times? Go, counsellor.
Thou and my bosom henceforth shall be twain.
I'll to the Friar to know his remedy.
If all else fail, myself have power to die.

[*Exit*]

things stand, I think it's best if you married the Count. Oh, he's a lovely gentleman. Romeo's a dishrag compared to him. An eagle, madam, doesn't have as green, as quick, as beautiful an eye as Paris has. A curse on my very heart if I'm wrong, but I think this second marriage is fortunate, because it's better than your first. Even if it isn't, your first husband's dead, or as good as dead, with him still living here on earth but you never seeing him.

Juliet Do you speak from your heart?

Nurse And from my soul too, or else a curse on them both.

Juliet Amen.

Nurse What?

Juliet Well, you've been a wonderful comfort to me. Go and tell my mother that I've gone to Friar Lawrence to make a confession and receive forgiveness, because I displeased my father.

Nurse Indeed I will. This is the wise thing to do.

[*The* **Nurse** *exits*]

Juliet You cursed old woman! You wicked fiend! Is it more sinful to urge me to break my marriage vows, or to criticize my husband with the same tongue she used to praise him beyond compare so many thousand times? Go, adviser! You'll never hear my private thoughts again. I'll go to the Friar to see what he suggests. If all else fails, I have the power to kill myself.

[**Juliet** *exits*]

Comprehension   Check What You Know

1. Review the interactions among the characters in Scene 1. Which characters seem to want to fight most? Which ones seem to want peace?

2. What does Mercutio mean when he says, "I have it, and soundly, too. Your houses!" (Scene 1, line 104)? What happens to him?

3. What is Romeo's mood when he enters the action in Scene 1? How and why does his mood change? What does he mean when he says, "O, I am fortune's fool" in line 133 of the scene?

4. What does Juliet express about Tybalt? What is the source of her conflicting emotions?

5. What does Friar Lawrence report to Romeo? How does he counsel Romeo about being a man?

6. What plans are hurried by Capulet and Lady Capulet?

7. How does Juliet respond to her father in Scene 5?

8. Describe the emotions in the Capulet home at the end of this act.

Activities & Role-Playing   Classes or Informal Groups

ID the Pairs   Work with a group. Review the characters in the play. Each person in the group identifies an event or a character and a second member of the group names an opposite or a counterpart. For example, one member might say "Montague" and a second member might say "Capulet." Refer to the list of the characters in this text and also recall events in the play so far. (Examples: Juliet is in the balcony; Romeo is below the balcony. Hatred and love are opposed.)

Gary Sloan as Mercutio, Derek D. Smith as Romeo, Edward Gero as Tybalt with company in The Shakespeare Theatre's production of *Romeo and Juliet* directed by Michael Kahn. Photo by Joan Marcus.

More Than Just a Scratch Role-play Act 3's first scene. Imagine the immediate tension on the open streets. Consider the mocking remarks and insults that the two groups trade. Be sure to include the sarcasm and physical action of this scene. Reflect on how quickly matters can get out of hand when loyalties are so very strong.

Discussion Classes or Informal Groups

1. Discuss Mercutio's behavior. Do you think he would make a good friend? Why or why not? How responsible is he for what happens in Scene 1?

2. Compare Romeo's experiences with his friends and when he's with Juliet. What is he like when he is with her? What is he like without her?

3. Juliet experiences many different emotions in Scene 2. Discuss how it might feel to go back and forth between two very different sets of emotions. What might that do to your sense of whether you were thinking clearly?

4. Discuss Friar Lawrence and his relationship with Romeo. How helpful is he to Romeo? What do you think of his questions about Romeo's manhood in Scene 3 (lines 116–166)?

5. Discuss the exchange between Juliet and her parents. How might you feel if you were Juliet?

Suggestions for Writing Improve Your Skills

1. Write a chronology of the events in the play so far. Determine a date for the first act and list the action from there. For each day, write a short summary of the events for that day. How does the mood of the action change with the time of day?

2. Research Phoebus and Phaeton in encyclopedias or other references that tell you about these characters from Greek myths. Compare the meaning of these characters with the action of this act. What relationship can you find between the two? Write footnotes that you think might be helpful for parts of Scene 2. Note the scene and line number where you think the footnote might be placed to help explain this reference to Greek mythology.

3. Review Juliet's conversation with her mother in Scene 5 (lines 71–128). Note any double meanings that Juliet uses. Write a brief essay explaining what you think these double meanings show about Juliet's character and her relationship with her parents.

4. Write an obituary for Mercutio and/or for Tybalt. Include information you can find about their families, friends, personalities, likes and dislikes, and favorite activities.

All the World's a Stage Introduction

Love conquers all, people say. But Romeo and Juliet's love faces harder and harder challenges. After killing Tybalt in a fury over Mercutio's murder, Romeo has been banished by Prince Escalus. Meanwhile, old Capulet has arranged a marriage for his lovely daughter—not realizing that Romeo and Juliet are already husband and wife. After one joyous night in each other's arms, the pair separates and Romeo heads for exile in the city of Mantua. Now, they hope time will be on their side—but Juliet's family has other plans.

What's in a Name? Characters

Romeo does not appear in Act 4. This gives us more time to examine his rival, Paris. On paper, he is a better match: a wealthy nobleman whose alliance with the Capulets could help the family "move up" in the world. If the Nurse is right, we know that Paris is also good-looking. Pay attention to Paris's speech and behavior where Juliet's concerned. Is he a sympathetic character or a villain?

Romeo's absence also lets the audience take a closer look at Juliet. In Act 4, this 14-year-old girl will make some important, adult decisions. What do you think of the choices she makes? How has her character changed since Act 1?

COME WHAT MAY Things to Watch For

The tension between what we *think* will happen and what we *want* to happen is one of the strange pleasures of watching a tragic play. To complicate matters even more, in Act 4 a *pretend* tragedy will occur! As Juliet struggles to preserve her happiness, she takes a serious risk to preserve her union with Romeo, but it could also make her the "bride of death." How does this metaphor reflect on the fates and characters of Juliet, Paris, and Romeo? Does it send a good or bad message for the happiness of Shakespeare's characters? How do you feel about Friar Lawrence's role in Juliet's decisions?

Has a coincidence ever changed your life? At the beginning of the play, the Prologue told us that Romeo and Juliet were "star-crossed lovers." Watch for the way a chance decision causes Romeo and Juliet even more problems in Scene 2. How else has good or bad luck affected their tale?

All Our Yesterdays Historical and Social Context

A traditional 21st-century wedding can be an expensive, complicated affair. The same was true in Shakespeare's day. Juliet's father seems to be planning an extremely elaborate wedding for Paris and his daughter. In Act 4, he'll hire twenty cooks for the bash! Nothing is too good for his daughter!

In Shakespeare's England, the average age of marriage was twenty-four for women and nearly twenty-seven for men. Members of the nobility often married when they were younger, but even so, Elizabethans would have regarded Juliet's marrying age of fourteen as extremely young. In the long poem that Shakespeare used as his source for the plot, Juliet is slightly older—sixteen. We don't know why Shakespeare made Juliet so young—perhaps he felt it added to the sense of an exotic Italian setting in the past, or perhaps the boy actor who played Juliet couldn't pass for an older girl. Whatever the reason, his choice made sure that generations of teens would identify with this love-struck pair.

The Play's the Thing Staging

Remember Peter, the Nurse's servant? This seemingly bit part was originally played by a great "star" of the Elizabethan stage, William Kempe. Kempe got his start as a jester. As a stage actor, he was a highly popular specialist—a clown. He seems to have been especially good at playing slapstick bumblers and at dancing the *jigs* that were traditionally performed at the ends of plays—including tragedies.

Today, most audiences would be surprised to see a jig at the end of a tension-filled play like *Romeo and Juliet*. A combination of comedy, singing, and dancing, jigs sent playgoers home on a note of very light comic and musical relief. Kempe had a talent for making up jigs, and he seems to have been well known for his energy and his silliness.

With a popular actor like Kempe on hand, Shakespeare had to write roles to fit his talents. Although Kempe was one of the founding partners in the Globe theater, he left Shakespeare's company shortly afterward. Some scholars theorize that Shakespeare's company had "outgrown" Kempe's jigs and ad-libs.

My Words Fly Up Language

Have you ever listened to people talk at a funeral? Did you notice how they used stock phrases and clichés to express sympathy? Near the end of Act 4, several characters react to what they believe is a tragedy. The Nurse, for example, cries "O woe! O woeful, woeful, day." It's unlike Shakespeare to load his lines with this kind of stilted repetition. But the language here tells us something about the way his characters react to the tragedy.

In the final scene, Peter taunts the musicians by calling them "Catling," "Rebeck," and "Soundpost"—names that refer to a lute string, a violin, and the inside of a stringed instrument, respectively. Worst of all, he calls them "minstrels," implying the music-makers are mere vagabonds.

211

Act IV

Scene I

Friar Lawrence's cell. Enter **Friar Lawrence** *and* **Paris**

Friar Lawrence On Thursday, sir? The time is very short.

Paris My father Capulet will have it so,
And I am nothing slow to slack his haste.

Friar Lawrence You say you do not know the lady's mind.
5   Uneven is the course. I like it not.

Paris Immoderately she weeps for Tybalt's death,
And therefore have I little talked of love,
For Venus smiles not in a house of tears.
Now sir, her father counts it dangerous
10   That she do give her sorrow so much sway,
And in his wisdom hastes our marriage
To stop the inundation of her tears
Which, too much minded by herself alone,
May be put from her by society.
15   Now do you know the reason of this haste.

Friar Lawrence I would I knew not why it should be slowed.
Look sir, here comes the lady toward my cell.

[*Enter* **Juliet**]

Paris Happily met, my lady and my wife.

Friar Lawrence's chamber. **Friar Lawrence** *and* **Paris** *enter.*

Friar Lawrence   On Thursday, sir? That's such a short time!

Paris   My father-in-law, Capulet, wishes it that way. And I have no desire to slow him down.

Friar Lawrence   You say you don't know the lady's thoughts on this? This matter is irregular. I don't like it.

Paris   She weeps to excess over Tybalt's death, so I haven't talked much of love. Venus, the goddess of love, doesn't smile in a house of tears. Her father thinks it's dangerous that she lets her sorrow overwhelm her. In his wisdom, he hastens our marriage to stop her great flow of tears. She thinks too much about her sorrow when she is alone. Being out among others may help her to forget her grief. Now you know the reason for this haste.

Friar Lawrence   [*to himself*] I wish I didn't know why it should be postponed! [*To* **Paris**] Look, sir, here comes the lady toward my chamber.

[**Juliet** *enters*]

Paris   What a happy meeting! My lady and my wife.

Juliet   That may be, sir, when I may be a wife.

20 **Paris**   That may be, must be, love, on Thursday next.

Juliet   What must be, shall be.

Friar Lawrence   That's a certain text.

Paris   Come you to make confession to this father?

Juliet   To answer that, I should confess to you.

25 **Paris**   Do not deny to him that you love me.

Juliet   I will confess to you that I love him.

Paris   So will ye, I am sure, that you love me.

Juliet   If I do so, it will be of more price
      Being spoke behind your back than to your face.

30 **Paris**   Poor soul, thy face is much abused with tears.

Juliet   The tears have got small victory by that,
      For it was bad enough before their spite.

Paris   Thou wrong'st it more than tears with that report.

Juliet   That is no slander, sir, which is a truth,
35   And what I spake, I spake it to my face.

Paris   Thy face is mine, and thou hast slandered it.

Juliet   It may be so, for it is not mine own.
      Are you at leisure, holy father, now,
      Or shall I come to you at evening mass?

40 **Friar Lawrence**   My leisure serves me, pensive daughter,
            now.
      My lord, we must entreat the time alone.

Paris   God shield I should disturb devotion.
      Juliet, on Thursday early will I rouse ye.
45   Till then, adieu and keep this holy kiss.

                                          [*Exit*]

Juliet That may be, sir, when I *am* a wife.

Paris That "may be" *must* be, my love, this Thursday.

Juliet What must be, shall be.

Friar Lawrence That's a true maxim.

Paris Do you come here to make confession to this father?

Juliet To answer that, I would be confessing to you.

Paris Don't deny to him that you love me.

Juliet I will confess to you that I love him.

Paris And also, I'm sure, that you love me?

Juliet If I did, it would be more valuable if it were spoken behind your back than to your face.

Paris Poor soul, your face is streaked with tears.

Juliet The tears have won a small victory by that. It was bad enough before the tears.

Paris When you say that, you do more wrong to your face than your tears did.

Juliet It's not a slander, sir, if it's the truth. What I said, I said concerning my face.

Paris Your face is mine, and you have slandered it.

Juliet That may be so, since it is not mine. Are you free now, holy Father, or shall I come to you at evening mass?

Friar Lawrence I'm free now, my heavy-hearted daughter. My lord, we must ask for time alone.

Paris God forbid that I should disturb religious devotions. Juliet, I'll call for you early on Thursday. Till then, farewell, and keep this holy kiss.

[**Paris** *exits*]

Juliet O shut the door, and when thou hast done so,
   Come weep with me, past hope, past cure, past help!

Friar Lawrence O Juliet, I already know thy grief;
   It strains me past the compass of my wits.
50   I hear thou must – and nothing may prorogue it –
   On Thursday next be married to this County.

Juliet Tell me not, Friar, that thou hearest of this,
   Unless thou tell me how I may prevent it.
   If in thy wisdom thou canst give no help,
55   Do thou but call my resolution wise,
   And with this knife I'll help it presently.
   God joined my heart and Romeo's, thou our hands;
   And ere this hand, by thee to Romeo's sealed,
   Shall be the label to another deed,
60   Or my true heart with treacherous revolt
   Turn to another, this shall slay them both.
   Therefore, out of thy long-experienced time
   Give me some present counsel, or behold:
   'Twixt my extremes and me this bloody knife
65   Shall play the umpire, arbitrating that
   Which the commission of thy years and art
   Could to no issue of true honour bring.
   Be not so long to speak. I long to die
   If what thou speak'st speak not of remedy.

70 **Friar Lawrence** Hold, daughter. I do spy a kind of hope
   Which craves as desperate an execution
   As that is desperate which we would prevent.
   If, rather than to marry County Paris,
   Thou hast the strength of will to slay thyself,
75   Then is it likely thou wilt undertake
   A thing like death to chide away this shame,
   That cop'st with death himself to scape from it.
   And if thou dar'st, I'll give thee remedy.

Juliet Oh, shut the door, and when you've done that, come and weep with me—past hope, past cure, past help!

Friar Lawrence Oh Juliet, I already know the cause of your grief. I'm at my wit's end! I hear you must marry the Count this Thursday, and that nothing can delay it.

Juliet Don't tell me that you've heard of this, Friar, unless you also tell me how I can prevent it. If in your wisdom you can give no help, then just tell me I'm making a wise decision, and I'll help myself at once with this knife. God joined my heart and Romeo's, and you joined our hands. Before this hand, which you sealed to Romeo's hand, shall seal another marriage contract, or before my faithful heart treacherously rebels and turns to someone else, this knife will kill them both. Therefore, from your past long experience, give me some advice now. Or watch: This deadly knife will play the umpire between my desperate situation and myself. It will decide what the authority of your years and your skill can't offer as an honorable solution. Speak quickly. I long to die, if what you speak offers no remedy.

Friar Lawrence Wait, daughter! I do see a kind of hope. It needs as desperate an action as the desperate event we want to prevent. Rather than marry Count Paris, you say you have the strength of will to kill yourself. It's likely, then, that you'll be able to undergo a thing *like* death to avoid this shame, since you would face Death himself to escape from it. If you dare, I'll give you a remedy.

Juliet O, bid me leap, rather than marry Paris,
80   From off the battlements of any tower,
    Or walk in thievish ways, or bid me lurk
    Where serpents are. Chain me with roaring bears,
    Or hide me nightly in a charnel-house
    O'ercovered quite with dead men's rattling bones,
85   With reeky shanks and yellow chapless skulls.
    Or bid me go into a new-made grave,
    And hide me with a dead man in his shroud –
    Things that, to hear them told, have made me tremble –
    And I will do it without fear or doubt.
90   To live an unstained wife to my sweet love.

Friar Lawrence Hold then. Go home, be merry, give consent
    To marry Paris. Wednesday is tomorrow;
    Tomorrow night look that thou lie alone.
    Let not the Nurse lie with thee in thy chamber.
95   Take thou this vial, being then in bed,
    And this distilling liquor drink thou off;
    When presently through all thy veins shall run
    A cold and drowsy humour, for no pulse
    Shall keep his native progress, but surcease;
100   No warmth, no breath shall testify thou livest,
    The roses in thy lips and cheeks shall fade
    To wanny ashes, thy eyes' windows fall
    Like death when he shuts up the day of life.
    Each part deprived of supple government
105   Shall stiff and stark and cold appear, like death,
    And in this borrowed likeness of shrunk death
    Thou shall continue two and forty hours
    And then awake as from a pleasant sleep.
    Now when the bridegroom in the morning comes
110   To rouse thee from thy bed, there art thou, dead.
    Then as the manner of our country is,
    In thy best robes, uncovered on the bier

Juliet Oh, tell me to leap from off the battlements of any tower, rather than marry Paris. Or walk in places infested with thieves. Tell me to wander where snakes are. Chain me with roaring bears. Hide me night after night in a mortuary, covered with dead men's rattling bones, with stinking limbs and yellow, jawless skulls. Tell me to go into a newly dug grave, and hide me with a dead man in his grave clothes—things that have made me tremble just to hear them said. I will do it without fear or doubt, to live a loyal wife to my sweet love.

Friar Lawrence Wait then. Go home, be cheerful, and agree to marry Paris. Tomorrow is Wednesday. Tomorrow night, be sure to sleep alone. Don't let the Nurse sleep with you in your bedroom. Take this little bottle. When you're in bed, drink all of the liquid in the bottle. Soon, a cold and drowsy fluid will flow through your veins. Your pulse will stop. No warmth, no breath will give a sign that you're alive. The rosiness in your lips and cheeks will fade to pale gray. Your eyelids will close, like death closes the day of life. Each part of you, losing control of movement, will appear stiff and stark and cold, like death. This death-like appearance will continue for forty-two hours. Then you'll awake as if from a pleasant sleep. When the bridegroom Paris comes in the morning to rouse you from your bed, there you'll be—dead. Then, as is customary in our country, you'll be dressed in your best robes and

Thou shall be borne to that same ancient vault
Where all the kindred of the Capulets lie.
115 In the meantime, against thou shalt awake,
Shall Romeo by my letters know our drift
And hither shall he come, and he and I
Will watch thy waking, and that very night
Shall Romeo bear thee hence to Mantua,
120 And this shall free thee from this present shame,
If no inconstant toy nor womanish fear
Abate thy valour in the acting it.

Juliet   Give me, give me! O tell not me of fear.

Friar Lawrence   Hold. Get you gone. Be strong and
125   prosperous
In this resolve. I'll send a friar with speed
To Mantua with my letters to thy lord.

Juliet   Love give me strength, and strength shall help afford.
Farewell, dear father.

[*Exeunt*]

carried uncovered on a funeral bier to the burial vault where all the Capulet family lies. In the meantime, in preparation for your awakening, I'll write to Romeo to let him know our plan. He'll come here, and he and I will be there when you awake. That very night, Romeo will take you to Mantua. You'll be free from your present shame, if you don't change your mind or if no womanish fear interferes with your courage in acting out the plan.

Juliet Give it to me! Give it to me! Oh, don't tell me about fear!

Friar Lawrence Here. [*He gives her the bottle*] Get going. Be strong and determined. I'll send a friar quickly to Mantua with my letters to your husband.

Juliet Love, give me strength, and strength will give me the help I need. Farewell, dear father.

[**Friar Lawrence** *and* **Juliet** *exit*]

Act IV

Scene II

Capulet's house. Enter **Capulet, Lady Capulet, Nurse** *and two or three* **Servants**

Capulet So many guests invite as here are writ.

[Exit **Servant***]*

Sirrah, go hire me twenty cunning cooks.

Servant You shall have none ill, sir, for I'll try if they can lick their fingers.

5   **Capulet** How canst thou try them so?

Servant Marry sir, 'tis an ill cook that cannot lick his own fingers; therefore he that cannot lick his fingers goes not with me.

Capulet Go, be gone.

[Exit **Servant***]*

10   We shall be much unfurnished for this time.
        What, is my daughter gone to Friar Lawrence?

Nurse Ay, forsooth.

Capulet Well, he may chance to do some good on her.
        A peevish self-willed harlotry it is.

Capulet's house. **Capulet, Lady Capulet,** *the* **Nurse,** *and* **Servants** *enter.*

Capulet [*to a* **Servant**] Invite the guests whose names are written on this list.

[*The* **Servant** *exits*]

You, man, go hire me twenty skilled cooks.

Servant You won't get any bad ones, sir, for I'll test them by seeing if they can lick their fingers.

Capulet How does that test them?

Servant Well, sir, it's a bad cook who can't lick his own fingers. So if he can't lick his fingers, he won't come back with me.

Capulet Go on, then. Be off.

[*The* **Servant** *exits*]

We're very unprepared for this event. What? Has my daughter gone to Friar Lawrence?

Nurse Yes, in truth.

Capulet Well, he may do some good with her. A peevish, willful, worthless creature she is!

[*Enter* **Juliet**]

15 **Nurse** See where she comes from shrift with merry look.

Capulet How now, my headstrong: where have you
    been gadding?

Juliet Where I have learnt me to repent the sin
    Of disobedient opposition
20   To you and your behests, and am enjoined
    By holy Lawrence to fall prostrate here,
    To beg your pardon. Pardon, I beseech you.
    Henceforward I am ever ruled by you.

Capulet Send for the County, go tell him of this.
25   I'll have this knot knit up tomorrow morning.

Juliet I met the youthful lord at Lawrence' cell,
    And gave him what becomed love I might,
    Not stepping o'er the bounds of modesty.

Capulet Why, I am glad on't. This is well. Stand
30   up.
    This is as't should be. Let me see the County.
    Ay marry. Go, I say, and fetch him hither.
    Now afore God, this reverend Holy Friar,
    All our whole city is much bound to him.

35 **Juliet** Nurse, will you go with me into my closet,
    To help me sort such needful ornaments
    As you think fit to furnish me tomorrow?

Lady Capulet No, not till Thursday, there is time enough.

Capulet Go, Nurse, go with her. We'll to church
40   tomorrow.

[*Exeunt* **Juliet** *and* **Nurse**]

[**Juliet** *enters*]

Nurse Look, she comes from confession with a cheerful look.

Capulet Well now, my headstrong girl: Where have you been wandering?

Juliet Where I've learned to be sorry for the sin of disobediently opposing you and your commands. I've been told by the holy Lawrence to fall down in front of you to beg your pardon. Pardon, I beg you. From now on, I'll always be ruled by you.

Capulet Send for the Count. Tell him of this. I'll have this marriage knot tied up tomorrow morning!

Juliet I met the young lord at Lawrence's cell, and gave him such love as was befitting, without stepping over the bounds of modesty.

Capulet Well, I'm glad of it. This is well! Stand up! This is as it should be. I want to see the Count. Yes, I say! Go, I say, and fetch him here. Now before God, our whole city is much indebted to this reverend Holy Friar.

Juliet Nurse, will you go with me to my room to help me choose the things you think I'll need to wear tomorrow?

Lady Capulet No, not till Thursday. There's time enough.

Capulet Go, Nurse, go with her. We'll go to church tomorrow.

[**Juliet** *and the* **Nurse** *exit*]

Lady Capulet We shall be short in our provision,
'Tis now near night.

Capulet   'Tush I will stir about,
And all things shall be well, I warrant thee, wife.
45 Go thou to Juliet, help to deck up her.
I'll not to bed tonight, let me alone.
I'll play the housewife for this once. What ho!
They are all forth. Well, I will walk myself
To County Paris, to prepare up him
50 Against tomorrow. My heart is wondrous light
Since this same wayward girl is so reclaimed.

                              [*Exeunt*]

Lady Capulet We won't have enough food and drink. It's almost night.

Capulet Tush, I'll get things going. Everything will be fine, I promise you, wife. You go to Juliet. Help to get her ready. I won't be going to bed tonight. Leave it to me. I'll play the housewife for this once. [*Calling his servants*] Hello, there! They're all out. Well, I'll walk to Count Paris myself, to prepare him for tomorrow. I'm very lighthearted since my wayward girl has been set straight.

[**Capulet** *and* **Lady Capulet** *exit*]

Act IV

Scene III

Juliet's bedroom. Enter **Juliet** *and* **Nurse**

Juliet Ay, those attires are best. But, gentle Nurse,
I pray thee leave me to myself tonight,
For I have need of many orisons
To move the heavens to smile upon my state,
5   Which, well thou know'st, is cross and full of sin.

[*Enter* **Lady Capulet**]

Lady Capulet What, are you busy, ho? Need you my help?

Juliet No madam. We have culled such necessaries
As are behoveful for our state tomorrow.
So please you, let me now be left alone
10   And let the Nurse this night sit up with you,
For I am sure you have your hands full all
In this so sudden business.

Lady Capulet   Good night.
Get thee to bed and rest, for thou hast need.

[*Exeunt* **Lady Capulet** *and* **Nurse**]

15   **Juliet** Farewell. God knows when we shall meet again.
I have a faint cold fear thrills through my veins,
That almost freezes up the heat of life.
I'll call them back again to comfort me.
Nurse! What should she do here?
20   My dismal scene I needs must act alone.
Come vial.

228

Juliet's bedroom. **Juliet** *and the* **Nurse** *enter.*

Juliet   Yes, those clothes are the best. Gentle Nurse, please leave me alone tonight. I need many prayers to encourage the heavens to smile upon my soul—which, as you well know, is stubborn and full of sin.

[**Lady Capulet** *enters*]

Lady Capulet   What, are you busy? Do you need my help?

Juliet   No madam. We've picked out the things necessary for the ceremony tomorrow. So if you please, let me be left alone now, and let the Nurse sit up with you tonight. I'm sure you have your hands full, with this sudden business.

Lady Capulet   Good night. Go to bed and rest, for you need it.

[**Lady Capulet** *and the* **Nurse** *exit*]

Juliet   Farewell. God knows when we'll meet again. A feeling of faint, cold fear pierces my veins, that almost freezes me to death. I'll call them back again to comfort me. Nurse! What could she do here? I must act out this dreadful scene alone. Come, little bottle. What if this mixture doesn't work at all?

What if this mixture do not work at all?
Shall I be married then tomorrow morning?
No, no. This shall forbid it. [*She lays down her knife*]

25   Lie thou there.
What if it be a poison which the Friar
Subtly hath ministered to have me dead,
Lest in this marriage he should be dishonoured
Because he married me before to Romeo?
30 I fear it is; and yet methinks it should not,
For he hath still been tried a holy man.
How if, when I am laid into the tomb,
I wake before the time that Romeo
Come to redeem me? There's a fearful point!
35 Shall I not then be stifled in the vault,
To whose foul mouth no healthsome air breathes in,
And there die strangled ere my Romeo comes?
O, if I live, is it not very like
The horrible conceit of death and night,
40 Together with the terror of the place –
As in a vault, an ancient receptacle,
Where, for this many hundred years, the bones
Of all my buried ancestors are packed;
Where bloody Tybalt yet but green in earth.
45 Lies festering in his shroud; where, as they say,
At some hours in the night spirits resort –
Alack, alack! Is it not like that I,
So early waking, what with loathsome smells
And shrieks like mandrakes torn out of the earth,
50 That living mortals, hearing them run mad –
O, if I wake shall I not be distraught,
Environed with all these hideous fears,
And madly play with my forefathers' joints,
And pluck the mangled Tybalt from his shroud.
55 And in this rage, with some great kinsman's bone,
As with a club, dash out my desperate brains?
O look! Methinks I see my cousin's ghost,
Seeking out Romeo that did spit his body
Upon a rapier's point. Stay, Tybalt, stay!
60 Romeo, I come! This do I drink to thee.

[*She falls on her bed*]

Shall I be married then tomorrow morning? No! No! This will prevent it. [*She takes out her knife*] You lie there. [*She puts it beside the bed*] What if it's a poison that the Friar has cleverly given me to kill me, in case this marriage should bring dishonor to him because he married me before to Romeo? I fear it is. And yet I think it isn't, since he's always proved himself a holy man. What if, when I'm laid in the tomb, I wake before Romeo comes to claim me? That's a frightening point! Wouldn't I then be smothered in the vault, which never gets fresh air, and die strangled there before my Romeo comes? Or, if I live, isn't it likely that horrible ideas of death and night, together with the terror of the place—it is a vault, an ancient tomb, where for hundreds of years the bones of all my buried ancestors are stored; where bloody Tybalt newly buried lies rotting in his shroud; where, they say, at certain hours in the night, ghosts walk. . . . Alas, alas! Isn't it likely that I, waking too early—what with the loathsome smells and shrieks like mandrakes torn out of the ground, which make living beings go mad when they hear them. . . . Oh, if I wake, won't I go mad, surrounded by all these hideous fears, and play with my ancestors' bones like a madwoman? Won't I pluck the mangled Tybalt from his shroud? And, in this madness, won't I use some great ancestor's bone like a club to dash out my desperate brains? Oh, look! I think I see my cousin's ghost, looking for Romeo, who stuck his body upon a dagger's point. Stop, Tybalt, stop! Romeo, I come! I drink this for you.

[*She falls on her bed*]

Act IV

Scene IV

The hall in Capulet's house. Enter **Lady Capulet** *and* **Nurse**

Lady Capulet Hold, take these keys and fetch more spices, Nurse.

Nurse They call for dates and quinces in the pastry.

[*Enter* **Capulet**]

Capulet Come, stir, stir, stir! The second cock hath crowed,
5   The curfew bell hath rung, 'tis three o'clock.
Look to the baked meats, good Angelica;
Spare not for cost.

Nurse   Go, ye cot-quean, go.
Get you to bed. Faith, you'll be sick tomorrow
10   For this night's watching.

Capulet No, not a whit. What! I have watched ere now
All night for lesser cause and ne'er been sick.

Lady Capulet Ay, you have been a mouse-hunt in your time.
But I will watch you from such watching now.

[*Exeunt* **Lady Capulet** *and* **Nurse**]

15 **Capulet** A jealous hood, a jealous hood!

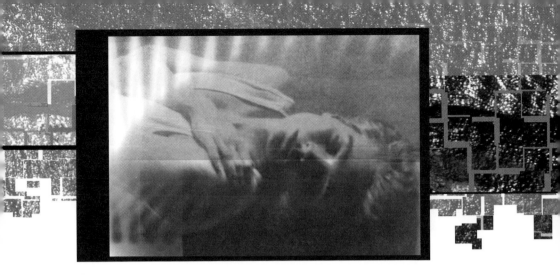

The hall in Capulet's house. **Lady Capulet** *and the* **Nurse** *enter.*

Lady Capulet Here, take these keys and fetch more spices, Nurse.

Nurse They're asking for dates and quinces in the pastry room.

[**Capulet** *enters*]

Capulet Come on—move! move! move! Two roosters have crowed, the curfew bell has rung—it's three o'clock in the morning. See about the baked meats, good Nurse. Don't spare the cost.

Nurse Go on, you man playing housewife, go on. Get yourself to bed. By my faith, you'll be sick tomorrow from staying awake tonight.

Capulet No, not a bit. What! I've stayed awake all night before, for less reason, and never been sick.

Lady Capulet Yes, you've been a woman-chaser in your time. But I'll stay awake to keep you from those kinds of late nights now!

[**Lady Capulet** *and the* **Nurse** *exit*]

Capulet A jealous woman, a jealous woman!

[*Enter three or four* **Servants** *with spits and logs and baskets*]

Now fellow, what is there?

First Servant   Things for the cook, sir, but I know not what.

Capulet   Make haste, make haste!

[*Exit* **First Servant**]

Sirrah, fetch drier logs!
20   Call Peter, he will show thee where they are.

Second Servant   I have a head, sir, that will find out logs
And never trouble Peter for the matter.

Capulet   Mass and well said! A merry whoreson, ha!
Thou shalt be loggerhead!

[*Exit* **Second Servant**]

25   Good faith! 'Tis day!
The County will be here with music straight,
For so he said he would. I hear him near.
Nurse! Wife! What ho! What, Nurse, I say!

[*Enter* **Nurse**]

Go waken Juliet, go, and trim her up.
30   I'll go and chat with Paris. Hie, make haste,
Make haste! The bridegroom he is come already.
Make haste I say.

[*Exeunt*]

[**Servants** *enter with meat-spits, logs, and baskets*]

Now fellow, what do you have there?

First Servant   Things for the cook, sir, but I don't know what.

Capulet   Hurry up, hurry up!

[**First Servant** *exits*]

You, man, fetch drier logs! Call Peter. He'll show you where they are.

Second Servant   I've got a good head, sir, for finding logs. I don't have to bother Peter about it.

Capulet   Good! Well said! A witty chap! You'll be called "blockhead"!

[**Second Servant** *exits*]

Good grief! It's day! The Count will be here with musicians any time now. He said he would. I hear him coming! Nurse! Wife! Hello there! What, Nurse, I say!

[*The* **Nurse** *enters*]

Go and wake up Juliet, go on. Dress her up. I'll go and chat with Paris. Hurry! Hurry! The bridegroom's here already. Hurry up, I say!

[**Capulet** *and the* **Nurse** *exit*]

Act IV
Scene V

Juliet's bedroom. Enter **Nurse**

Nurse Mistress! What, mistress! Juliet! Fast, I warrant her,
    she.
    Why, lamb! why, lady! Fie, you slugabed!
    Why, love, I say! Madam! Sweetheart! Why, bride!
5   What, not a word? You take your pennyworths now.
    Sleep for a week; for the next night, I warrant,
    The County Paris hath set up his rest
    That you shall rest but little! God forgive me!
    Marry and amen. How sound is she asleep!
10   I needs must wake her. Madam, madam, madam!
    Ay, let the County take you in your bed,
    He'll fright you up, i'faith. Will it not be?
    What, dressed, and in your clothes, and down again?
    I must needs wake you. Lady! Lady! Lady!
15   Alas, alas! Help, help! My lady's dead!
    O well-a-day that ever I was born.
    Some aqua vitae, ho! My lord! My lady!

[*Enter* **Lady Capulet**]

Lady Capulet What noise is here?

Nurse   O lamentable day!

20 **Lady Capulet** What is the matter?

Nurse   Look, look! O heavy day!

Juliet's bedroom. The **Nurse** *enters.*

Nurse Mistress! Mistress! Juliet! Fast asleep, I'll bet. Why lamb! My lady! Ha! You slugabed! Why, love, I say! Madam! Sweetheart! Bride! What, not a word? You take your little bit of rest now. Sleep for a week! For tomorrow night, I'll bet, Count Paris has resolved not to give you any rest. God forgive me! Amen! How sound asleep she is! I must wake her. Madam! Madam! Madam! Yes, let the Count find you in your bed, and he'll scare you out of it, by my faith. Won't you be up? What, dressed, and in your clothes, and lying back down again? I must wake you! Lady! Lady! Lady! Alas! Alas! Help! Help! My lady's dead! Oh, alas! Woe the day that I was ever born! Some brandy here! My lord! My lady!

[**Lady Capulet** *enters*]

Lady Capulet What's all the noise here?

Nurse Oh mournful day!

Lady Capulet What's the matter?

Nurse Look! Look! Oh sorrowful day!

Lady Capulet O me, O me! My child, my only life.
Revive, look up, or I will die with thee.
Help, help! Call help!

[*Enter* **Capulet**]

25 **Capulet** For shame, bring Juliet forth, her lord is come.

Nurse She's dead, deceased! She's dead! Alack the day!

Lady Capulet Alack the day! She's dead, she's dead, she's
dead!

Capulet Ha! Let me see her. Out alas. She's cold,
30 Her blood is settled and her joints are stiff.
Life and these lips have long been separated.
Death lies on her like an untimely frost
Upon the sweetest flower of all the field.

Nurse O lamentable day!

35 **Lady Capulet**   O woeful time!

Capulet Death, that hath ta'en her hence to make me wail
Ties up my tongue and will not let me speak.

[*Enter* **Friar Lawrence** *and* **Paris** *and* **Musicians**]

Friar Lawrence Come, is the bride ready to go to church?

Capulet Ready to go, but never to return.
40 O son, the night before thy wedding day
Hath Death lain with thy wife. There she lies,
Flower as she was, deflowered by him.
Death is my son-in-law, Death is my heir.
My daughter he hath wedded. I will die,
45 And leave him all: life, living, all is Death's.

Lady Capulet Oh me! Oh me! My child! My only life! Wake up, look up, or I'll die with you! Help! Help! Call help!

[**Capulet** *enters*]

Capulet For shame! Bring Juliet out here. Her bridegroom has come.

Nurse She's dead! Lifeless! She's dead! Alas the day!

Lady Capulet Alas the day! She's dead! She's dead! She's dead!

Capulet What! Let me see her! Oh no, alas! She's cold. Her blood has settled. Her limbs are stiff. Life and these lips have long been separated. Death lies on her like a late frost upon the sweetest flower in all the field.

Nurse Oh sorrowful day!

Lady Capulet Oh woeful time!

Capulet Death, who has taken her to make me wail in grief, ties my tongue and won't let me speak.

[**Friar Lawrence, Paris,** *and the* **Musicians** *enter*]

Friar Lawrence Come, is the bride ready to go to church?

Capulet Ready to go, but she'll never return. Oh son—on the night before your wedding day, Death slept with your wife. There she lies, flower that she was, deflowered by Death. Death is my son-in-law. Death is my heir. He has married my daughter. I will die, and leave him everything: life, property, everything is Death's.

Paris Have I thought long to see this morning's face,
And doth it give me such a sight as this?

Lady Capulet Accursed, unhappy, wretched, hateful day.
Most miserable hour that e'er time saw
50   In lasting labour of his pilgrimage.
But one, poor one, one poor and loving child,
But one thing to rejoice and solace in,
And cruel Death hath catched it from my sight.

Nurse O woe! O woeful, woeful, woeful day.
55   Most lamentable day! Most woeful day
That ever, ever I did yet behold.
O day, O day, O day, O hateful day.
Never was seen so black a day as this.
O woeful day, O woeful day.

60 **Paris** Beguiled, divorced, wronged, spited, slain,
Most detestable Death, by thee beguiled,
By cruel, cruel, thee, quite overthrown.
O love, O life, not life, but love in death.

Capulet Despised, distressed, hated, martyred, killed.
65   Uncomfortable time, why cam'st thou now
To murder, murder our solemnity?
O child, O child! My soul and not my child,
Dead art thou. Alack, my child is dead,
And with my child my joys are buried.

70 **Friar Lawrence** Peace, ho, for shame. Confusion's cure lives
    not
In these confusions. Heaven and yourself
Had part in this fair maid, now heaven hath all,
And all the better is it for the maid.
75   Your part in her you could not keep from death,
But heaven keeps his part in eternal life.
The most you sought was her promotion,
For 'twas your heaven she should be advanced,
And weep ye now, seeing she is advanced

Paris Have I been so impatient to see this morning arrive, to have it give me such a sight as this?

Lady Capulet Cursed, unhappy, wretched, hateful day! Most miserable hour that Time has ever known. Just one child, one poor child, one poor and loving child. The one thing that I rejoiced and took comfort in, and cruel Death has snatched her from my sight.

Nurse Oh sorrow! Oh woeful, woeful, woeful day. Most sorrowful day. Most mournful day that I have ever, ever yet seen. Oh day, oh day, oh day, oh hateful day! There was never such a black day as this! Oh woeful day, oh woeful day!

Paris Deceived, divorced, wronged, spited, murdered! Deceived by you, detestable Death! Quite ruined by you, cruel, cruel Death! Oh love! Oh life! Not alive, but still loved in death.

Capulet Despised, distressed, hated, martyred, killed. Comfortless time, why did you come now to murder, murder our festivity? Oh child, oh child! My soul—not my child—you are dead! Alas, my child is dead, and my joys are buried with my child.

Friar Lawrence Quiet, for shame! There's no cure for loss in crying and wailing. Heaven and yourselves both had a part of this beautiful maid. Now heaven has all of her, and the maid is all the better for it. You couldn't keep your part of her from death, but heaven keeps its part of her in eternal life. The most that you wanted to gain for her was her advancement. Your idea of heaven for her was that she should marry well. And yet you weep now, seeing that she is advanced above the clouds, as high as heaven itself? Oh, in mourning for her like this now, you love your child so little that you go crazy, seeing

80   Above the clouds, as high as heaven itself?
        O, in this love you love your child so ill
        That you run mad, seeing that she is well.
        She's not well married that lives married long,
        But she's best married that dies married young.
85   Dry up your tears, and stick your rosemary
        On this fair corse, and, as the custom is,
        All in her best array bear her to church.
        For though fond nature bids us all lament,
        Yet nature's tears are reason's merriment.

90   **Capulet** All things that we ordained festival
        Turn from their office to black funeral:
        Our instruments to melancholy bells,
        Our wedding cheer to sad burial feast,
        Our solemn hymns to sullen dirges change,
95   Our bridal flowers serve for a buried corse,
        And all things change them to the contrary.

        Friar Lawrence Sir, go you in, and madam, go with him,
        And go, Sir Paris. Everyone prepare
        To follow this fair corse unto her grave.
100   The heavens do lour upon you for some ill;
        Move them no more by crossing their high will.

        [*Exeunt all but the* **Nurse** *and* **Musicians,** *casting rosemary
        on* **Juliet** *and shutting the curtains*]

        First Musician Faith, we may put up our pipes and be gone.

        Nurse Honest good fellows, ah put up, put up,
        For well you know this is a pitiful case.

105   **First Musician** Ay, by my troth, the case may be amended.

        [*Exit* **Nurse**]

that she is well off. Being married a long time doesn't mean one has married well. She that dies married young is the best married. Dry your tears. Place your rosemary, for remembrance, on this fair corpse. According to custom, dress her in her best clothes and carry her to church. For though our foolish human nature makes us mourn, our reason mocks our emotional tears.

Capulet All the things that we intended to be festive must now be turned black for a funeral. The music will turn into melancholy bells; our wedding banquet will be a sad burial feast; our solemn hymns will change to mournful funeral dirges; our bridal flowers will serve for the buried corpse. All things will be changed to their opposite.

Friar Lawrence Sir, you go now, and madam, go with him. And go, Sir Paris. Everyone prepare to follow this fair corpse to her grave. The heavens frown upon you for some evil thing you've done. Don't anger them any further by antagonizing them.

[*All exit except the **Nurse** and **Musicians**. The herb rosemary is placed on **Juliet** and the curtains are closed*]

First Musician By my faith, we must put away our instruments and be gone.

Nurse Good fellows, yes, pack up, pack up. You can easily see that this is a pitiful case.

First Musician Yes, in truth, the case could be better than it is.

[*The **Nurse** exits*]

[*Enter* **Peter**]

Peter   Musicians, O musicians, 'Heart's ease', 'Heart's ease'!
O, and you will have me live, play 'Heart's ease'.

First Musician   Why 'Heart's ease'?

Peter   O musicians, because my heart itself plays 'My heart is
110   full'. O play me some merry dump to comfort me.

First Musician   Not a dump we! 'Tis no time to play now.

Peter   You will not then?

First Musician   No.

Peter   I will then give it you soundly.

115   **First Musician**   What will you give us?

Peter   No money, on my faith, but the gleek! I will give you the
minstrel.

First Musician   Then will I give you the serving-creature.

Peter   Then will I lay the serving-creature's dagger on your
120   pate. I will carry no crotchets. I'll re you, I'll fa you. Do you
note me?

First Musician   And you re us and fa us, you note us.

Second Musician   Pray you put up your dagger and put out
your wit.

125   **Peter**   Then have at you with my wit. I will dry-beat you with
an iron wit, and put up my iron dagger. Answer me like men.

'When griping griefs the heart doth wound,
And doleful dumps the mind oppress,
Then music with her silver sound' –

130   Why 'silver sound'? Why 'music with her silver sound'?
What say you, Simon Catling?

[**Peter** *enters*]

Peter Musicians, oh, musicians! Play "Heart's Ease"! "Heart's Ease"! If you want me to keep living, play "Heart's Ease"!

First Musician Why "Heart's Ease"?

Peter Oh, musicians, because my heart itself is playing "My Heart Is Full." Oh, play me some cheery mournful tune to comfort me.

First Musician We won't play a mournful tune! This is no time for us to play.

Peter You won't, then?

First Musician No.

Peter Then I'll give it to you, soundly!

First Musician What will you give us?

Peter Not money, by my faith, but a sneer! I'll call you "minstrels"!

First Musician Then I'll call you what you are, a servant!

Peter [*Takes out his dagger*] Then I'll use my servant's dagger to knock you on the head. I won't endure your insults! I'll "re" you! I'll "fa" you! Do you note what I'm telling you?

First Musician If you "re" us and "fa" us, you note us!

Second Musician Please, put away your dagger and pull out your wit and intelligence.

Peter Then I'll go after you with my wit! I'll beat you with merciless iron wit and put away my iron dagger. Answer me like men [*he quotes from an old song*]:

> When griping griefs the heart doth wound,
> And doleful dumps the mind oppress,
> Then music with her silver sound—

Why "silver sound"? Why "music with her silver sound"? What do you say, Simon Catling?

First Musician Marry, sir, because silver hath a sweet sound.

Peter Pretty. What say you, Hugh Rebeck?

Second Musician I say 'silver sound' because musicians
135   sound for silver.

Peter Pretty too. What say you, James Soundpost?

Third Musician Faith, I know not what to say.

Peter O, I cry you mercy, you are the singer. I will say for you.
It is 'music with her silver sound' because musicians have no
140   gold for sounding.

   'Then music with her silver sound
   With speedy help doth lend redress.'

[Exit]

First Musician What a pestilent knave is this same.

Second Musician Hang him, Jack. Come, we'll in here, tarry
145   for the mourners, and stay dinner.

[Exeunt]

First Musician Well, sir, because silver has a sweet sound.

Peter Pretty good! What do you say, Hugh Rebeck?

Second Musician I say "silver sound" because musicians are paid in silver coins for making sounds.

Peter Pretty good, too! What do you say, James Soundpost?

Third Musician Faith, I don't know what to say.

Peter Oh, I beg your pardon. You're the singer. I'll say it for you. It's "music with her silver sound" because musicians don't get paid gold for playing.

> Then music with her silver sound
> With speedy help does lend redress.

> [**Peter** *exits*]

First Musician What a miserable scoundrel he is!

Second Musician Hang him, Jack. Come on, we'll go in here, wait for the mourners, and stay for dinner.

> [*They exit*]

Comprehension   Check What You Know

1. What secret do the Friar and Juliet share that Paris does not know?

2. Review the scene between Paris and Juliet. Compare Juliet's behavior when she is with Romeo and when she is with Paris.

3. Describe Juliet's state of mind in Scene 1.

4. What does the Friar give to Juliet?

5. What is Lady Capulet busy preparing?

6. Summarize Juliet's speech at the end of Scene 3.

7. Describe Capulet and Lady Capulet in Scene 4. What is the mood of the household?

8. What does the Nurse report to Capulet in Scene 5? What has Juliet done?

Activities & Role-Playing   Classes or Informal Groups

Two Faces Review Juliet's and Friar Lawrence's roles in their scenes in this act. Write brief *soliloquies* for scenes 1, 2, and 3. (A *soliloquy* is a speech that a character says to himself or herself, revealing his or her private thoughts. See Juliet's speech at the end of Scene 3.) For your soliloquies, include the secret information that Juliet and the Friar know but do not share with others in the scene. After the original lines, add "but I know . . ." or "but I am really going to. . . ." Role-play these scenes and include the extra lines of these secrets.

Cooks in a Kitchen Refer to encyclopedias or other resources to learn about food and preparations for fancy weddings in Shakespeare's time. Create a menu listing the ingredients (herbs, meats, and so forth). Assign a recipe to each person in your group and reenact the wedding preparations by the servants.

Discussion Classes or Informal Groups

1. What do you think of Paris? What admirable qualities does he have? How would you feel if you were Paris?

2. Discuss the Friar's advice to Juliet. Is he a reliable source of information? What do you think of his advice to Juliet?

3. Compare the Nurse's feelings when she finds Juliet with Lady Capulet's reactions. How close is the Nurse to Juliet?

4. Discuss the final scene with the musicians. How have the events shifted in the work they will do? How difficult or easy might it be to change the music they will be playing?

5. Discuss Juliet's actions. What do you think of what she has done? Is it selfish? Why might you empathize with (or feel sorry for) her?

Suggestions for Writing Improve Your Skills

1. Juliet's speech in Scene 3 (lines 15–60) includes many images of earth and tombs. Identify other imagery in this speech. Write an essay describing the images Juliet uses to explain her state of mind at this point in the play.

2. The mood of Act 4 shifts many times. Find examples of happiness, sadness, desperation, frustration, and other emotions in this act. Review each scene. Imagine you are the director. Write a list of directing notes for each scene that you will use to guide your actors. List the emotions and mannerisms that you want the characters to convey for each scene. For example, for Scene 1 you might write: Happiness (Paris), Secrecy (Friar, Juliet).

3. Review the lines spoken by Peter and the musicians and compare them to the lines spoken by Capulet or the Friar. How has Shakespeare written lines differently for aristocratic or educated people versus common people? Note the differences and write one or two paragraphs explaining why you think Shakespeare wrote in two different ways.

All the World's a Stage Introduction

Will love or hatred triumph? As Act 5 opens, Romeo lives in exile in Mantua. Juliet lies in a tomb. She has faked her own death in a desperate attempt to reunite with the young man she secretly married. If all goes as the lovers plan, they will live happily ever after. If they fail, the punishment will be harsh.

Are Romeo and Juliet tragically heroic figures? Or are they thoughtless and selfish? Shakespeare's audiences may have rooted for Romeo and Juliet while at the same time questioning the lovers' judgment. In Elizabethan England, people did not think of individual rights as we do today, and they had a very strong sense of how family and national history shaped their own lives. Between 1553 and 1558, two half-sisters, Mary (a Catholic) and Elizabeth (a Protestant), had battled for control of the throne of England. The rebellions, confrontations, and bloody executions ultimately led to Elizabeth becoming Queen, but they had brought misery to everyone in England.

So the idea of a private world of love must have appealed to some Elizabethans. Others may have thought that Romeo and Juliet were fools, trying to live out a fantasy. They might even have viewed the lovers as dangerously irresponsible. What will happen when this marriage is revealed?

What's in a Name? Characters

In *Romeo and Juliet*, Verona is almost a character itself. It suffers, protests, and watches as the Montague and Capulet gangs tear up its streets. Today, we sometimes think of the warfare between gang "families" as modern problems. Like the people of Shakespeare's Verona, we long for the "good old days" when everyone behaved themselves—or so we think!

Prince Escalus and a group of citizens speak for Verona. Escalus has been the voice of law and order in the play, and we have seen the fighting families judged in citizens' public opinion. In Acts 1 and 3, they condemned the disorderly families harshly. In Act 5, Escalus and the citizens will finally get to judge and hear the full story. Now that the lovers' tale is finally out in the open, does it gain new meaning?

COME WHAT MAY Things to Watch For

As Mercutio died, he called for "a plague o' both your houses!" Was this a prophecy? In the play's final act, watch for images of plagues and scourges to see how Mercutio's words do and don't come true.

Plague tore through Europe during Shakespeare's time. The disease caused great suffering, but in some ways it enforced order. In times of plague, people stayed in their homes and authorities banned public gatherings to keep the disease from spreading. In London, theaters were shut down for months during epidemics. Death left the streets and stages empty.

All Our Yesterdays **Historical and Social Context**

In Act 5, Romeo visits an apothecary. The closest modern-day example may be a pharmacist. And like today's drugstores, apothecaries also sold items like candy, perfumes, and beauty aids. However, Shakespeare's apothecary is very different from the friendly pharmacist at your local drugstore. Apothecaries mixed their "medicines" in their shops, instead of receiving them from a manufacturer. The remedies ranged from medicinal herbs to illegal potions, fake cures like ground unicorn's horn and newt's liver, and poisons. Apothecaries also sold aphrodisiacs—love potions that would guarantee the love and desire of anyone who ingested the potion.

Some medical doctors today frown upon the healing claims of "herbalists." Likewise, the physicians who tried to regulate medical practice in Shakespeare's England thought apothecaries were dangerous nuisances. But people patronized them anyway.

The Play's the Thing **Staging**

What is a tragedy? In earlier eras, some critics complained that "The Tragedy of Romeo and Juliet" wasn't a tragedy at all. They felt that Shakespeare's plot relied too much on accidents and coincidence. They said that real tragedies involved fate, not chance, and terrible inner flaws that drove characters to make tragic choices. For others, Shakespeare's story was *too* tragic, so they altered Act 5 to add more cheerful notes. In the 18th century, *Romeo and Juliet* might feature a fancy funeral for the drugged Juliet, after which she awakened to converse with Romeo in the burial vault.

Today, some of these changes might sound silly. But it's also dangerous to treat Shakespeare like a sacred cow. Stage directors frequently fiddle with Shakespeare's settings and characters, trying to present the plays in fresh ways. How would you change or retell *Romeo and Juliet*?

My Words Fly Up **Language**

When Juliet first met Romeo, she told him, "You kiss by the book." Even before that, Romeo's friends made fun of his by-the-book sighs as he pined for Rosaline. They thought his love relied on formulas because it wasn't real.

In Act 5, pay attention to how Romeo speaks. His language is less fanciful—in some ways, it's less "pretty." How else has he changed? Shakespeare's language changes, too. Notice how his lines rhyme less and move more fluidly from line to line than in the play's first scenes. This is also the style of the great plays he wrote after *Romeo and Juliet*—plays like *Hamlet* and *Macbeth*. Did the author grow up with his teenage lovers?

Act V

Scene I

A street in Mantua. Enter **Romeo**

Romeo If I may trust the flattering truth of sleep
    My dreams presage some joyful news at hand.
    My bosom's lord sits lightly in his throne
    And all this day an unaccustomed spirit
5   Lifts me above the ground with cheerful thoughts.
    I dreamt my lady came and found me dead –
    Strange dream that gives a dead man leave to think! –
    And breathed such life with kisses in my lips
    That I revived and was an emperor.
10   Ah me, how sweet is love itself possessed
    When but love's shadows are so rich in joy.

[*Enter* **Balthazar,** *Romeo's man*]

    News from Verona! How, now Balthasar,
    Dost thou not bring me letters from the Friar?
    How doth my lady? Is my father well?
15   How doth my Juliet? That I ask again,
    For nothing can be ill if she be well.

Balthazar Then she is well and nothing can be ill.
    Her body sleeps in Capels' monument,
    And her immortal part with angels lives.
20   I saw her laid low in her kindred's vault
    And presently took post to tell it you.
    O pardon me for bringing these ill news,
    Since you did leave it for my office, sir.

A street in Mantua. **Romeo** *enters.*

Romeo If I can trust these favorable dreams to be true, joyful news is on its way. My love gently rules my heart, and all day today I've felt an unusual lightheartedness that makes me feel like I'm walking on air. I dreamed my lady came and found me dead—a strange dream that allows a dead man to think! And she breathed such life into me with kisses on my lips that I revived and was an emperor. Ah me, how sweet love is when you possess it in reality, considering how love's dreams are so rich in joy!

[**Balthazar,** *Romeo's servant, enters*]

News from Verona! Hello, Balthazar. Do you bring me letters from the Friar? How is my lady? Is my father well? How is Juliet? That I ask again, for nothing can be ill if she is well.

Balthazar Then she is well, and nothing can be ill. Her body sleeps in the Capulets' family vault, and her immortal soul lives with angels. I saw her laid down in her family's vault, and I immediately hired post-horses to come and tell you about it. Pardon me for bringing this bad news. It was my responsibility, sir, which you left with me.

Romeo Is it e'en so? Then I defy you, stars!
25   Thou know'st my lodging. Get me ink and paper,
And hire posthorses. I will hence tonight.

Balthazar I do beseech you sir, have patience.
Your looks are pale and wild and do import
Some misadventure.

30 **Romeo**   Tush, thou art deceived.
Leave me, and do the thing I bid thee do.
Hast thou no letters to me from the Friar?

Balthazar No, my good lord.

Romeo   No matter. Get thee gone.
35   And hire those horses. I'll be with thee straight.

[*Exit* **Balthazar**]

Well, Juliet, I will lie with thee tonight.
Let's see for means. O mischief thou art swift
To enter in the thoughts of desperate men.
I do remember an apothecary –
40   And hereabouts a dwells – which late I noted
In tattered weeds, with overwhelming brows,
Culling of simples. Meagre were his looks.
Sharp misery had worn him to the bones,
And in his needy shop a tortoise hung,
45   And alligator stuffed, and other skins
Of ill-shaped fishes; and about his shelves
A beggarly account of empty boxes,
Green earthen pots, bladders, and musty seeds,
Remnants of packthread, and old cakes of roses
50   Were thinly scattered to make up a show.
Noting this penury, to myself I said,
'And if a man did need a poison now,
Whose sale is present death in Mantua,
Here lives a caitiff wretch would sell it him'.

Romeo Is it really so? Then I defy you, Fate! You know where I live. Get me ink and paper, and hire post-horses. I'll leave tonight.

Balthazar I beg you sir, bear this patiently. You look pale and wild, and you could have an accident or a misfortune in your condition.

Romeo Nonsense! Don't be fooled by my appearance. Leave me, and do what I told you to do. Don't you have any letters to me from the Friar?

Balthazar No, my good lord.

Romeo It doesn't matter. Go on. Hire those horses. I'll be with you soon.

[**Balthazar** *exits*]

Well, Juliet, I'll lie with you tonight. Let's see what means I can use. How quickly desperate men's thoughts turn to desperate deeds! I remember an apothecary—who lives around here—whom I saw recently, in tattered clothes, with jutting brows, gathering medicinal herbs. He looked thin and poor. Misery had worn him down to the bones. In his poor shop a tortoiseshell hung, and a stuffed alligator, and other skins of odd-looking fishes. Thinly spread around his shelves to make a show were a few empty boxes, green earthenware pots, leather bottles, old seeds, pieces of string, and old blocks of pressed rose petals. Noting his poverty, I said to myself, "If a man needed poison, which you can be executed for selling in Mantua, here is the evil man who would sell it to him."

55 O, this same thought did but forerun my need,
And this same needy man must sell it me.
As I remember, this should be the house.
Being holiday, the beggar's shop is shut.
What ho! Apothecary!

[*Enter* **Apothecary**]

60 **Apothecary**   Who calls so loud?

Romeo Come hither man. I see that thou art poor.
Hold, there is forty ducats. Let me have
A dram of poison, such soon-spreading gear
As will disperse itself through all the veins,
65 That the life-weary taker may fall dead,
And that the trunk may be discharged of breath
As violently as hasty powder fired
Doth hurry from the fatal cannon's womb.

Apothecary Such mortal drugs I have, but Mantua's law
70 Is death to any he that utters them.

Romeo Art thou so bare and full of wretchedness,
And fear'st to die? Famine is in thy cheeks,
Need and oppression starveth in thy eyes,
Contempt and beggary hangs upon thy back.
75 The world is not thy friend, nor the world's law;
The world affords no law to make thee rich;
Then be not poor, but break it, and take this.

Apothecary My poverty, but not my will consents.

Romeo I pay thy poverty and not thy will.

80 **Apothecary** Put this in any liquid thing you will
And drink it off and if you had the strength
Of twenty men it would dispatch you straight.

Oh, that very thought foreshadowed my need. Now this same needy man must sell it to me. As I remember, this should be the house. Being a holiday, the beggar's shop is closed. Hello there! Apothecary!

[*The* **Apothecary** *enters*]

Apothecary   Who calls so loud?

Romeo   Come here, man. I see you're poor. Look. Here's forty gold coins. Let me have a small bottle of poison, quick-working stuff that will spread itself through all the veins so that the life-weary suicide will fall dead, his body expelling his breath as violently as gunpowder exploding from a cannon.

Apothecary   I have such deadly drugs, but Mantua's law calls for the death sentence to any man who sells them.

Romeo   Are you so poor and full of wretchedness, and yet afraid to die? Starvation shows in your cheeks. Need and worry show in your eyes. Beggary and contempt hang on your back. The world isn't your friend, nor is the world's law. The world offers no law that will make you rich. So don't be poor. Break the law and take this.

Apothecary   My poverty, not my will, agrees.

Romeo   I'm paying your poverty, not your will.

Apothecary   Put this in any liquid you wish, and drink it down. Even if you had the strength of twenty men, it would kill you immediately.

Romeo There is thy gold – worse poison to men's souls,
Doing more murder in this loathsome world
85   Than these poor compounds that thou mayst not sell.
I sell thee poison, thou hast sold me none.
Farewell, buy food, and get thyself in flesh.
Come cordial, and not poison, go with me
To Juliet's grave, for there must I use thee.

[*Exeunt*]

Romeo Here's your gold—worse poison to men's soul. It causes more murder in this hateful world than these miserable mixtures that you're not allowed to sell. I sell you poison; you haven't sold any to me. Goodbye. Buy food and get some flesh on your bones. Come, healing medicine—not poison—and go with me to Juliet's grave. There I must use you.

[**Romeo** *and the* **Apothecary** *exit*]

Act V

Scene II

Friar Lawrence's cell. Enter **Friar John**

Friar John   Holy Franciscan Friar, Brother, ho!

[*Enter* **Friar Lawrence**]

Friar Lawrence   This same should be the voice of Friar John.
Welcome from Mantua. What says Romeo?
Or, if his mind be writ, give me his letter.

5 **Friar John**   Going to find a barefoot brother out,
One of our order, to associate me,
Here in this city visiting the sick,
And finding him, the searchers of the town,
Suspecting that we both were in a house
10   Where the infectious pestilence did reign,
Sealed up the doors and would not let us forth,
So that my speed to Mantua there was stayed.

Friar Lawrence   Who bare my letter then to Romeo?

Friar John   I could not send it – here it is again –
15   Nor get a messenger to bring it thee,
So fearful were they of infection.

Friar Lawrence   Unhappy fortune! By my brotherhood,
The letter was not nice but full of charge,
Of dear import, and the neglecting it

Friar Lawrence's cell. **Friar John** *enters.*

Friar John   Holy Franciscan Friar! Brother! Hello!

[**Friar Lawrence** *enters*]

Friar Lawrence   That's the voice of Friar John. Welcome back from Mantua! What does Romeo say? Or if he's written, give me his letter.

Friar John   I went to find a fellow Friar, a Franciscan, to go with me. He was here in the city visiting the sick. When I found him, health officials suspected that we both were in a house contaminated by the plague. They sealed up the doors and wouldn't let us out. So I was prevented from going to Mantua.

Friar Lawrence   Then who took my letter to Romeo?

Friar John   I couldn't send it—here it is back. I couldn't get a messenger to bring it to you, either, because they were so afraid of infection.

Friar Lawrence   What terrible fortune! By my holy brotherhood, this letter wasn't unimportant chitchat; it contained very important instructions. Not carrying out these instructions

20   May do much danger. Friar John, go hence,
         Get me an iron crow and bring it straight
         Unto my cell.

    Friar John   Brother I'll go and bring it thee.

                                                    [Exit]

    Friar Lawrence Now must I to the monument alone.
25   Within this three hours will fair Juliet wake.
         She will beshrew me much that Romeo
         Hath had no notice of these accidents,
         But I will write again to Mantua,
         And keep her at my cell till Romeo come.
30   Poor living corse, closed in a dead man's tomb.

                                                  [Exit]

could cause much harm. Friar John, go and get an iron crowbar, and bring it to my cell right away.

Friar John Brother, I'll go and bring it to you.

[**Friar John** *exits*]

Friar Lawrence Now I must go to the burial vault alone. Fair Juliet will awaken within three hours. She'll take me to task for Romeo's not getting notice of what has happened. But I'll write to Romeo again in Mantua, and keep her at my cell until he comes. Poor living corpse, locked in a dead man's tomb!

[**Friar Lawrence** *exits*]

Act V

Scene III

*The Capulets' vault. Enter **Paris** and his **Page***

Paris Give me the torch, boy. Hence and stand aloof.
Yet put it out, for I would not be seen.
Under yond yew trees lay thee all along,
Holding thy ear close to the hollow ground;
5   So shall no foot upon the churchyard tread,
Being loose, unfirm, with digging up of graves,
But thou shalt hear it. Whistle then to me
As a signal that thou hear'st something approach.
Give me those flowers. Do as I bid thee. Go.

10 **Page** I am almost afraid to stand alone
Here in the churchyard. Yet I will adventure.

[Retires]

*[**Paris** strews the tomb with flowers]*

Paris Sweet flower, with flowers thy bridal bed I strew.
O woe, thy canopy is dust and stones
Which with sweet water nightly I will dew,
15   Or wanting that, with tears distilled by moans.
The obsequies that I for thee will keep
Nightly shall be to strew thy grave and weep.

*[**Page** whistles]*

The Capulets' burial vault. **Paris** *and his* **Page** *enter.*

Paris   Give me the torch, boy. Go and stand at a distance. Wait—
put it out. I don't want to be seen. Lay down under the yew
trees over there, and hold your ear close to the hollow ground.
The ground is loose and not well packed from the digging up
of graves, so you'll hear any footstep in the churchyard.
Whistle to me as a signal if you hear someone approach.
Give me those flowers. Now go, do as I said.

Page   I'm almost afraid to stand alone here in the churchyard.
But I'll take my chances.

[*The* **Page** *hides*]

[**Paris** *scatters flowers over Juliet's tomb*]

Paris   Sweet flower! I scatter flowers on your bridal bed. Oh
sorrow! The canopy of your bed is dust and stones, over
which I'll sprinkle perfumed water every night. Or if not that,
I'll sprinkle tears of sorrow. The mourning rites that I will
keep for you will be to scatter flowers on your grave and
weep every night.

[*The* **Page** *whistles*]

The boy gives warning something doth approach.
What cursed foot wanders this way tonight,
20   To cross my obsequies and true love's rite?
What, with a torch? Muffle me, night, awhile.

[**Paris** *retires*]

[*Enter* **Romeo** *and* **Balthazar** *with a torch, a mattock and a crow of iron*]

Romeo Give me that mattock and the wrenching iron.
    Hold, take this letter. Early in the morning
    See thou deliver it to my lord and father.
25   Give me the light. Upon thy life I charge thee,
    Whate'er thou hear'st or seest, stand all aloof
    And do not interrupt me in my course.
    Why I descend into this bed of death
    Is partly to behold my lady's face
30   But chiefly to take thence from her dead finger
    A precious ring, a ring that I must use
    In dear employment. Therefore hence, be gone.
    But if thou jealous dost return to pry
    In what I farther shall intend to do,
35   By heaven I will tear thee joint by joint,
    And strew this hungry churchyard with thy limbs.
    The time and my intents are savage-wild,
    More fierce and more inexorable far
    Than empty tigers or the roaring sea.

40 **Balthazar** I will be gone, sir, and not trouble ye.

Romeo So shalt thou show me friendship. Take thou that.
    Live and be prosperous, and farewell, good fellow.

Balthazar For all this same, I'll hide me hereabout.
    His looks I fear, and his intents I doubt.

[**Balthazar** *retires*]

The boy is warning that someone is approaching. What cursed foot wanders this way tonight, interfering with my mourning and the rites of true love? What! With a torch! Hide me awhile, night.

[**Paris** *hides*]

[**Romeo** *and* **Balthazar** *enter with a torch and tools*]

Romeo Give me the pick and the crowbar. Here, take this letter. Make sure you deliver it early in the morning to my father. Give me the light. Upon your life, I order you—whatever you hear or see, stay back and don't interfere in what I'm doing. I'm entering this bed of death partly to see my lady's face, but mainly to remove a precious ring from her finger, a ring that I must use for a personal reason. So go on, but if you're suspicious and return to spy on what else I'm doing, by heaven I'll tear you limb from limb and scatter your limbs over this hungry churchyard. I'm in a savage state of mind right now—wild, more fierce, and more merciless by far than hungry tigers or the roaring sea!

Balthazar I'll be gone, sir, and not bother you.

Romeo That's how you can show me your friendship. [*He gives* **Balthazar** *some money*] Take that. Live and be prosperous. Farewell, good fellow.

Balthazar [*to himself*] All the same, I'll hide close by. I'm worried about how he looks, and I suspect his intentions.

[**Balthazar** *hides*]

45 **Romeo** Thou detestable maw, thou womb of death
     Gorged with the dearest morsel of the earth,
     Thus I enforce thy rotten jaws to open,
     And in despite I'll cram thee with more food.

[**Romeo** *opens the tomb*]

Paris This is that banished haughty Montague
50   That murdered my love's cousin – with which grief
     It is supposed the fair creature died –
     And here is come to do some villainous shame
     To the dead bodies. I will apprehend him.
     Stop thy unhallowed toil, vile Montague.
55   Can vengeance be pursued further than death?
     Condemned villain, I do apprehend thee.
     Obey, and go with me, for thou must die.

Romeo I must indeed, and therefore came I hither.
     Good gentle youth, tempt not a desperate man.
60   Fly hence and leave me. Think upon these gone.
     Let them affright thee. I beseech thee, youth,
     Put not another sin upon my head
     By urging me to fury. O be gone.
     By heaven I love thee better than myself,
65   For I come hither armed against myself.
     Stay not, be gone, live, and hereafter say
     A mad man's mercy bid thee run away.

Paris I do defy thy conjuration
     And apprehend thee for a felon here.

70 **Romeo** Wilt thou provoke me? Then have at thee, boy!

[*They fight*]

Page O Lord, they fight! I will go call the Watch.

[*Exit* **Page**]

Romeo You detestable stomach, you womb of death, gorged with the dearest morsel of earth! I'll force your rotten jaws to open, and in spite I'll cram you with more food.

[**Romeo** *opens the tomb*]

Paris This is that banished arrogant Montague who murdered my love's cousin. It's believed that she died from grief at this murder. He's come here to do something shameful to the dead bodies. I'll arrest him. [*He comes forward*] Stop your unholy work, you vile Montague! Can vengeance be pursued even after death? Condemned villain! I arrest you! Obey me, and come with me, for you must die!

Romeo I must indeed, and that's why I came here. Good gentle young man, don't tempt a desperate man. Run, and leave me. Think about these who are departed. Be frightened by them. I beg you, young man, don't cause me to add another sin on my head by pushing me to anger. Go on! By heaven, I love you better than I love myself, since I come here armed against myself. Don't stay. Go, live, and afterward you can say a madman's mercy caused you to run away.

Paris I refuse your appeal, and I arrest you as a criminal here!

Romeo Will you provoke me? Then have at it, boy!

[*They fight*]

Page Oh Lord, they fight! I'll go call the night watchmen!

[*The* **Page** *exits*]

Paris O, I am slain! If thou be merciful,
Open the tomb, lay me with Juliet.

[**Paris** *dies*]

Romeo In faith I will. Let me peruse this face.
75   Mercutio's kinsman, noble County Paris!
What said my man, when my betossed soul
Did not attend him, as we rode? I think
He told me Paris should have married Juliet.
Said he not so? Or did I dream it so?
80   Or am I mad, hearing him talk of Juliet,
To think it was so? O, give me thy hand,
One writ with me in sour misfortune's book.
I'll bury thee in a triumphant grave.
A grave? O no, a lantern, slaughtered youth.
85   For here lies Juliet, and her beauty makes
This vault a feasting presence, full of light.
Death, lie thou there, by a dead man interred.
How oft when men are at the point of death
Have they been merry! Which their keepers call
90   A lightning before death. O how may I
Call this a lightning? O my love, my wife,
Death that hath sucked the honey of thy breath
Hath had no power yet upon thy beauty.
Thou art not conquered. Beauty's ensign yet
95   Is crimson in thy lips and in thy cheeks,
And Death's pale flag is not advanced there.
Tybalt, liest thou there in thy bloody sheet?
O, what more favour can I do to thee
Than with that hand that cut thy youth in twain
100   To sunder his that was thine enemy?
Forgive me, cousin. Ah, dear Juliet,
Why art thou yet so fair? Shall I believe
That unsubstantial Death is amorous,
And that the lean abhorred monster keeps

Paris Oh, I'm killed! If you are merciful, open the tomb and lay
me beside Juliet.

[**Paris** *dies*]

Romeo By my faith, I will. Let me look at your face. Mercutio's
kinsman, noble Count Paris! What was it my servant said as
we rode here, when my mind was so upset I didn't pay
attention to him? I think he told me Paris was to have
married Juliet. Didn't he say that? Or did I dream it? Or am I
mad, hearing him talk of Juliet, and thinking it was so? Give
me your hand. Your name is written in bitter misfortune's
book, as is mine. I'll bury you in a magnificent grave. A
grave? Oh no, a glass tower, murdered youth. For here lies
Juliet, and her beauty makes this vault a room for a festival,
full of light. Death, lie there, buried by a dead man! How
often, when men are at the point of death, do they feel
happy! Their jailers call it a "lightening" before death. How
can I call it a lightening? Oh my love, my wife! Death, which
has sucked the honey of your breath, has had no power over
your beauty. You are not conquered. Beauty's sign is still
there in the crimson of your lips and your cheeks. Death's
pale flag has not been raised there. Tybalt! Is that you lying
there in your bloody shroud? What more of a favor can I do
for you than to cut down the one who was your enemy with
the same hand that shortened your youth? Forgive me,
cousin. Ah dear Juliet, why are you so beautiful? Should I
believe that bodiless Death is a lover, and that the lean,
horrible monster keeps you here in the dark to be his

105   Thee here in dark to be his paramour?
      For fear of that I still will stay with thee,
      And never from this palace of dim night
      Depart again. Here, here, will I remain
      With worms that are thy chambermaids. O here
110   Will I set up my everlasting rest
      And shake the yoke of inauspicious stars
      From this world-wearied flesh. Eyes, look your last.
      Arms, take your last embrace! And lips, O you
      The doors of breath, seal with a righteous kiss
115   A dateless bargain to engrossing Death.
      Come, bitter conduct, come unsavoury guide,
      Thou desperate pilot now at once run on
      The dashing rocks thy seasick weary bark.
      Here's to my love! [*He drinks*] O true apothecary,
120   Thy drugs are quick. Thus with a kiss I die.

                                            [*He falls*]

[*Enter **Friar Lawrence** with lantern, crow and spade*]

Friar Lawrence Saint Francis be my speed. How oft tonight
    Have my old feet stumbled at graves. Who's there?

Balthazar Here's one, a friend, and one that knows you well.

Friar Lawrence Bliss be upon you. Tell me, good my friend,
125   What torch is yond that vainly lends his light
    To grubs and eyeless skulls? As I discern,
    It burneth in the Capels' monument.

Balthazar It doth so, holy sir, and there's my master,
    One that you love.

130 **Friar Lawrence** Who is it?

Balthazar   Romeo.

Friar Lawrence How long hath he been there?

mistress? For fear of that, I'll stay with you forever and never again leave this palace of dim night. Here! Here I'll remain, with worms for my chambermaids. Here I'll set up my everlasting rest, and shake off from this world-weary body the burden of unfavorable stars. Eyes, look for the last time. Arms, take your last embrace! And lips, you doors of breath, seal with a pure kiss an endless contract with all-possessing Death. Come, bitter escort. Come, unpleasant guide, you desperate pilot. Now run your weary ship, sick of the sea, and dash it on the rocks. Here's to my love. [*He drinks the poison*] Oh honest apothecary! Your drugs are quick. With a kiss, I die.

[**Romeo** *dies*]

[**Friar Lawrence** *enters with a lantern, crowbar, and spade*]

Friar Lawrence Saint Francis, give me speed! How often tonight have my old feet stumbled on graves. Who's there?

Balthazar It's me, a friend, and one who knows you well.

Friar Lawrence Bless you. Tell me, my good friend, whose torch is that over there that wastes its light on worms and eyeless skulls? It looks to me like it burns in the Capulets' vault.

Balthazar It does, holy sir, and my master's there, the one you love.

Friar Lawrence Who is it?

Balthazar Romeo.

Friar Lawrence How long has he been there?

Balthazar   Full half an hour.

Friar Lawrence Go with me to the vault.

135 **Balthazar**   I dare not, sir.
    My master knows not but I am gone hence,
    And fearfully did menace me with death
    If I did stay to look on his intents.

Friar Lawrence Stay then, I'll go alone. Fear comes upon me.
140   O, much I fear some ill unthrifty thing.

Balthazar As I did sleep under this yew tree here
    I dreamt my master and another fought,
    And that my master slew him.

Friar Lawrence   Romeo!

[**Friar Lawrence** *stoops and looks on the blood and weapons*]

145   Alack, alack, what blood is this which stains
    The stony entrance of this sepulchre?
    What means these masterless and gory swords
    To lie discoloured by this place of peace?
    Romeo! O, pale! Who else? What, Paris too?
150   And steeped in blood? Ah what an unkind hour
    Is guilty of this lamentable chance?
    The lady stirs.

[**Juliet** *rises*]

Juliet O comfortable Friar, where is my lord?
    I do remember well where I should be,
155   And there I am. Where is my Romeo?

Friar Lawrence I hear some noise. Lady, come from that nest
    Of death, contagion, and unnatural sleep.
    A greater power than we can contradict
    Hath thwarted our intents. Come, come away.

Balthazar At least a half an hour.

Friar Lawrence Go with me to the vault.

Balthazar I don't dare, sir. My master thinks I'm gone, and he threatened me fearfully with death if I stayed to see what he was doing.

Friar Lawrence Stay then. I'll go alone. I feel fear coming over me. I'm very afraid that some unlucky thing has happened.

Balthazar As I slept under this yew tree here, I dreamed that my master and another person fought, and that my master killed him.

Friar Lawrence Romeo!

[**Friar Lawrence** *stoops to look at the blood and weapons*]

Alas, alas! Whose blood is this that stains the stones of the entrance to the vault? What's the meaning of these abandoned and bloody swords that lie near this place of peace? [*He goes into the vault*] Romeo! Oh, so pale! Who else? What? Paris too? And covered in blood? Ah, what cruel hour is responsible for this grievous coincidence? The lady stirs.

[**Juliet** *wakens*]

Juliet Oh, comforting Friar! Where is my husband? I do remember well where I should be—and here I am. Where is my Romeo?

Friar Lawrence I hear some noise. Lady, come from this nest of death, disease, and unnatural sleep. A greater power than we can oppose has destroyed our plans. Come, come away.

160 Thy husband in thy bosom there lies dead,
And Paris too. Come, I'll dispose of thee
Among a sisterhood of holy nuns.
Stay not to question, for the Watch is coming.
Come, go, good Juliet. I dare no longer stay.

165 **Juliet** Go get thee hence, for I will not away.

[*Exit* **Friar Lawrence**]

What's here? A cup closed in my true love's hand?
Poison, I see, hath been his timeless end.
O churl. Drunk all, and left no friendly drop
To help me after? I will kiss thy lips.
170 Haply some poison yet doth hang on them.
To make me die with a restorative. [*She kisses him*]
Thy lips are warm!

Watchman [*Outside*] Lead, boy. Which way?

Juliet Yea, noise? Then I'll be brief. O happy dagger.
175 This is thy sheath. There rust, and let me die.

[*She stabs herself and falls*]

[*Enter* **Page** *and* **Watchmen**]

Page This is the place. There, where the torch doth burn.

First Watchman The ground is bloody. Search about the
churchyard.
Go, some of you: whoe'er you find, attach.

[Ex*eunt some* **Watchmen**]

180 Pitiful sight! Here lies the County slain
And Juliet bleeding, warm, and newly dead,
Who here hath lain this two days buried.

Your husband lies dead in your arms. And Paris too. Come, I'll find a place for you in a convent of holy nuns. Don't ask questions. The night watchmen are coming. Come—go with me, good Juliet. I don't dare stay longer.

Juliet   Go, go away. I won't leave.

[**Friar Lawrence** *exits*]

What's this here? A cup closed in my true love's hand? Poison, I see, has been his untimely end. Oh miserly husband! Have you drunk all and left no friendly drop to help me follow after you? I'll kiss your lips. Perhaps some poison still hangs on them to make me die with a restoring medicine. Your lips are warm!

Watchman   [*outside*] Lead the way, boy. Which way?

Juliet   Do I hear noise? Then I'll be brief. Oh happy dagger! This is your sheath. Rust there, and let me die.

[*She stabs herself and falls*]

[**Page** *and* **Watchmen** *enter*]

Page   This is the place. There, where the torch burns.

First Watchman   The ground is bloody. Search around the churchyard. Go, some of you. Arrest whoever you find.

[*Some* **Watchmen** *exit*]

Pitiful sight! Here lies Count Paris, killed. And Juliet bleeding—warm and newly dead—who has lain here buried

Go tell the Prince. Run to the Capulets.
Raise up the Montagues. Some others search.

[*Exeunt some* **Watchmen**]

185 We see the ground whereon these woes do lie,
But the true ground of all these piteous woes
We cannot without circumstance descry.

[*Enter several* **Watchmen** *with* **Balthazar**]

Second Watchman   Here's Romeo's man. We found him in
the churchyard.

190 **First Watchman**   Hold him in safety till the Prince come
hither.

[*Enter another* **Watchman** *with* **Friar Lawrence**]

Third Watchman   Here is a friar that trembles, sighs and
weeps.
We took this mattock and this spade from him
195 As he was coming from this churchyard's side.

First Watchman   A great suspicion. Stay the friar too.

[*Enter the* **Prince** *and Attendants*]

Prince   What misadventure is so early up,
That calls our person from our morning rest?

[*Enter* **Capulet** *and* **Lady Capulet** *and Servants*]

Capulet   What should it be that is so shrieked abroad?

200 **Lady Capulet**   O, the people in the street cry 'Romeo',
Some 'Juliet', and some 'Paris', and all run
With open outcry toward our monument.

for these past two days. Go tell the Prince. Run to the Capulets. Call the Montagues. You others, search here.

[*Some* **Watchmen** *exit*]

We see the ground on which these pitiful bodies lie. But we can't find out the true reason for these woeful events until we have more details.

[*Several* **Watchmen** *enter with* **Balthazar**]

Second Watchman   Here's Romeo's servant. We found him in the churchyard.

First Watchman   Hold him securely until the Prince comes.

[*Another* **Watchman** *enters with* **Friar Lawrence**]

Third Watchman   Here's a friar—he trembles, sighs, and weeps. We took this pick and spade from him and he was coming from this side of the churchyard.

First Watchman   Very suspicious. Hold the friar, too.

[*The* **Prince** *and his attendants enter*]

Prince   What's the problem that calls us so early from our morning rest?

[**Capulet** *and* **Lady Capulet** *and servants enter*]

Capulet   What is it that everyone is shouting about?

Lady Capulet   People in the street cry "Romeo," some cry "Juliet," and some cry "Paris," and all run shouting toward our vault.

Prince What fear is this which startles in our ears?

First Watchman Sovereign, here lies the County Paris slain,
205   And Romeo dead, and Juliet, dead before,
    Warm, and new killed.

Prince Search, seek, and know how this foul murder comes.

First Watchman Here is a friar, and slaughtered Romeo's man,
    With instruments upon them fit to open
210   These dead men's tombs.

Capulet O heavens! O wife, look how our daughter bleeds!
    This dagger hath mista'en, for lo, his house
    Is empty on the back of Montague,
    And it mis-sheathed in my daughter's bosom.

215 **Lady Capulet** O me! This sight of death is as a bell
    That warns my old age to a sepulchre.

[*Enter* **Montague** *and Servants*]

Prince Come, Montague, for thou art early up
    To see thy son and heir now early down.

Montague Alas, my liege, my wife is dead tonight.
220   Grief of my son's exile hath stopped her breath.
    What further woe conspires against mine age?

Prince Look and thou shalt see.

Montague O thou untaught! What manners is in this,
    To press before thy father to a grave?

225 **Prince** Seal up the mouth of outrage for a while
    Till we can clear these ambiguities
    And know their spring, their head, their true descent,
    And then will I be general of your woes
    And lead you, even to death. Meantime forbear,
230   And let mischance be slave to patience.
    Bring forth the parties of suspicion.

Prince What's upsetting you all?

First Watchman Sovereign, here lies the Count Paris, killed. And Romeo dead, and Juliet, dead once before, now warm and newly killed.

Prince Search and find out how this foul murder happened!

First Watchman Here's a friar and slaughtered Romeo's servant, with tools on them fit to open these dead men's tombs.

Capulet Oh heavens! Oh wife! Look how our daughter bleeds! This dagger has made a mistake. For look, its sheath on that Montague's back is empty. It is mis-sheathed in my daughter's bosom!

Lady Capulet Oh me! This sight of death is like a bell calling my old age to a grave.

[**Montague** *and servants enter*]

Prince Come, Montague. You are up early, to see your son and heir now early down.

Montague Alas, my sovereign, my wife died tonight. Grief at my son's exile killed her. What further woe threatens my old age?

Prince Look and you shall see.

Montague Oh you untaught, rude boy! What bad manners is this, to go before your father to the grave?

Prince Control your passionate grief for a while, until we can clear up these mysteries and learn their source, their origin, their true beginnings. Then I'll take command and lead you in mourning, even to the death of the guilty. In the meantime, hold your grieving. Be patient in the face of misfortune. [*To the* **Watchmen**] Bring the suspects forward.

Friar Lawrence I am the greatest, able to do least,
　　　Yet most suspected, as the time and place
　　　Doth make against me, of this direful murder.
235　　And here I stand, both to impeach and purge
　　　Myself condemned and myself excused.

Prince Then say at once what thou dost know in this.

Friar Lawrence I will be brief, for my short date of breath
　　　Is not so long as is a tedious tale.
240　　Romeo, there dead, was husband to that Juliet,
　　　And she, there dead, that Romeo's faithful wife.
　　　I married them, and their stol'n marriage day
　　　Was Tybalt's doomsday, whose untimely death
　　　Banished the new-made bridegroom from this city;
245　　For whom, and not for Tybalt, Juliet pined.
　　　You, to remove that siege of grief from her,
　　　Betrothed and would have married her perforce
　　　To County Paris. Then comes she to me
　　　And with wild looks bid me devise some mean
250　　To rid her from this second marriage,
　　　Or in my cell there would she kill herself.
　　　Then gave I her – so tutored by my art –
　　　A sleeping potion, which so took effect
　　　As I intended, for it wrought on her
255　　The form of death. Meantime I writ to Romeo
　　　That he should hither come as this dire night
　　　To help to take her from her borrowed grave,
　　　Being the time the potion's force should cease.
　　　But he which bore my letter, Friar John,
260　　Was stayed by accident, and yesternight
　　　Returned my letter back. Then all alone
　　　At the prefixed hour of her waking
　　　Came I to take her from her kindred's vault,
　　　Meaning to keep her closely at my cell
265　　Till I conveniently could send to Romeo.
　　　But when I came, some minute ere the time

Friar Lawrence I'm the biggest suspect—able to do the least, yet the most suspected, because my being here at this time and place makes me appear guilty of this terrible murder. Here I stand, both to condemn myself for what I've done wrong and to clear myself of what may be excused.

Prince Then tell us immediately what you know about this.

Friar Lawrence I'll be brief, for my time left to live doesn't seem as long as a tedious tale. Romeo, there dead, was husband to Juliet. And she, there dead, was Romeo's faithful wife. I married them, and their secret wedding day was the day of Tybalt's death. His untimely death banished the new bridegroom from this city. It was for him, not for Tybalt, that Juliet mourned. [*To* **Capulet**] You, to end her grief, would have married her by force to Count Paris. Then she came to me and, terribly upset, asked me to figure out some way to save her from this second marriage, or she would kill herself right there in my cell. Then I gave her a sleeping potion—for I know that art. It worked as I expected, for it made her appear dead. Meantime, I wrote to Romeo that he should come here this very night to help take her from her temporary grave and be here by the time the potion wore off. But Friar John, who took my letter, was delayed by an accident, and last night he returned my letter to me. Then, at the prearranged time of her awakening, I came alone to take her from her family's vault. I intended to keep her secretly in my cell until I could conveniently send a letter to Romeo. But when I came,

Of her awakening, here untimely lay
The noble Paris and true Romeo dead.
She wakes, and I entreated her come forth
270 And bear this work of heaven with patience,
But then a noise did scare me from the tomb
And she, too desperate, would not go with me
But, as it seems, did violence on herself.
All this I know; and to the marriage
275 Her Nurse is privy; and if aught in this
Miscarried by my fault, let my old life
Be sacrificed some hour before his time
Unto the rigour of severest law.

Prince We still have known thee for a holy man.
280 Where's Romeo's man? What can he say to this?

Balthazar I brought my master news of Juliet's death,
And then in post he came from Mantua
To this same place, to this same monument.
This letter he early bid me give his father
285 And threatened me with death, going in the vault,
If I departed not and left him there.

Prince Give me the letter, I will look on it.
Where is the County's Page that raised the Watch?
Sirrah, what made your master in this place?

290 **Page** He came with flowers to strew his lady's grave
And bid me stand aloof, and so I did.
Anon comes one with light to ope the tomb
And by and by my master drew on him,
And then I ran away to call the Watch.

295 **Prince** This letter doth make good the Friar's words:
Their course of love, the tidings of her death,
And here he writes that he did buy a poison
Of a poor pothecary, and therewithal
Came to this vault to die and lie with Juliet.
300 Where be these enemies? Capulet, Montague,

just minutes before the time of her awakening, I found noble Paris and faithful Romeo dead. She awoke, and I pleaded with her to come out and bear heaven's will with patience, but then a noise scared me from the tomb. And she, too upset, would not leave with me, but it seems she did violence to herself instead. This is all I know. Her Nurse knows about the marriage. If anything in this went wrong because of me, let my old life be sacrificed before its time, according to the rigor of the severest law.

Prince We always have known you as a holy man. Where's Romeo's servant? What can he say about this?

Balthazar I brought my master news of Juliet's death, and then he hastily came from Mantua, here to this vault. He told me to give this letter to his father early in the morning. As he went into the vault, he threatened me with death if I didn't go and leave him there.

Prince Give me the letter. I'll look at it. Where is the Count's page who called the watchmen? Servant, what was your master doing in this place?

Page He came with flowers to strew on his lady's grave, and he told me to stand at a distance, so I did. Pretty soon someone came with a light to open the tomb, and by and by my master drew on him. Then I ran away to call the watchmen.

Prince This letter makes good the Friar's words: the course of their love, the news of her death. And here he writes that he bought a poison from a poor apothecary and came with it to this vault to die and lie with Juliet. Where are these enemies?

See what a scourge is laid upon your hate,
That heaven finds means to kill your joys with love;
And I, for winking at your discords too,
Have lost a brace of kinsmen. All are punished.

305 **Capulet** O brother Montague, give me thy hand.
This is my daughter's jointure, for no more
Can I demand.

Montague   But I can give thee more,
For I will raise her statue in pure gold,
310 That whiles Verona by that name is known,
There shall no figure at such rate be set
As that of true and faithful Juliet.

Capulet As rich shall Romeo's by his lady's lie,
Poor sacrifices of our enmity.

315 **Prince** A glooming peace this morning with it brings.
The sun for sorrow will not show his head.
Go hence to have more talk of these sad things.
Some shall be pardoned, and some punished,
For never was a story of more woe
320 Than this of Juliet and her Romeo.

[*Exeunt*]

Capulet, Montague: See what a curse is laid on your hate. Heaven finds means to kill your children with love. And I, for ignoring your quarrels, too have lost two relatives. We all are punished.

Capulet   O brother Montague, give me your hand. This handshake is my daughter's wedding gift from you: I can ask no more.

Montague   But I can give you more, for I'll put up a statue of her of pure gold. As long as Verona is known by that name, no figure shall be as valued as the true and faithful Juliet.

Capulet   And I'll place a statue of Romeo, just as rich, next to his lady's. These are the pitiful victims of our hatred.

Prince   This morning brings a gloomy kind of peace. The sun, in sorrow, will not show his face. Go now and talk about these sad things. Some will be pardoned and some punished. There never was a story of more woe, than this of Juliet and her Romeo.

[*They exit*]

Comprehension   Check What You Know

1. What does Romeo learn from Balthazar?

2. Why does Romeo meet with the Apothecary? What is he asking the Apothecary to provide?

3. Describe Romeo's state of mind. What does he plan to do?

4. Why wasn't the Friar's letter delivered to Romeo? Why is this so important in the events of Act 5?

5. What is in Romeo's letter to his father?

6. Why is Paris upset when he sees Romeo? What happens to Paris?

7. Romeo's final speech serves as a summary of his last thoughts. What does he tell the audience about love and death?

8. How does Juliet reenter the play? What does she learn about Romeo? What does she do next?

9. Describe the Montagues and Capulets and their reaction to the deaths of their children. What does Montague do? What does Capulet do?

Activities & Role-Playing   Classes or Informal Groups

Moving Among the Tombs   Create a model of the set for Scene 3. Include the Capulet vault, flowers, and other objects or props used in this scene. Reenact the events of this scene using small objects or models to represent the characters. Note how closely the action unfolds among the different sets of characters. Imagine finding the death and tragedy among the other tombs and graves in the churchyard.

©Hulton-Deutsch Collection/CORBIS

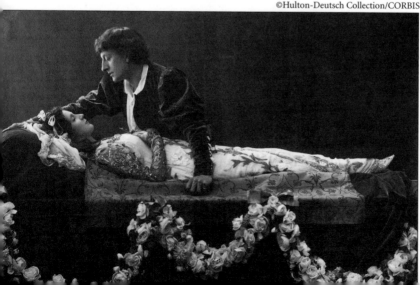

Young Love When you go to a play, the usher hands you a *playbill* that tells you about the play and the production. Gather playbills by visiting a theater or researching on the Internet. Create the cover and interior illustrations of a playbill for a production of *Romeo and Juliet.* In your design, represent the positive and negative characteristics of young love as portrayed in the play.

Discussion   Classes or Informal Groups

1. What makes *Romeo and Juliet* a tragic play?

2. Discuss suicide and why Juliet and Romeo are drawn to this end. Could they have made a different choice?

3. How do the adults affect the actions of Romeo and Juliet? Are the adults in any way responsible?

4. What do you think of Romeo's exchange with the Apothecary? Which events in the play may have ended differently? What moments hold great significance or meaning in the final actions of Romeo and Juliet?

5. What do you think of the Friar's last speech?

6. How have Romeo and Juliet become more mature? What changed them? How have they changed other people?

7. Who has suffered more—Romeo or Juliet?

8. Discuss the hate and love that run through the entire play. How does the play end? What is gained? What is lost?

Suggestions for Writing   Improve Your Skills

1. At the beginning of the play, the Chorus described Romeo and Juliet as "star-crossed lovers." Find horoscopes in a newspaper or magazine and study the way they give advice by watching the stars. Based on the events in this play, write a horoscope for Juliet and one for Romeo. What kinds of emotions or people would you warn them to avoid? Who or what would you suggest they trust? What days or times would you say were lucky or unlucky?

2. Research the city of Verona at the library or on the Internet. Find examples of how Verona pays tribute to the legend of Romeo and Juliet. Write a tour guide summarizing your findings and include photocopies of photographs.

3. Write a diary entry for the Prince in which he summarizes the events of Act 5. Include any predictions about what he thinks will happen between the Capulets and the Montagues in the future.

Romeo and Juliet
Additional Resources

Books

Title: *The Riverside Shakespeare*
Author: J. J. M. Tobin et al. (editors)
Publisher: Houghton Mifflin
Year: 1997
Summary: This volume features all of Shakespeare's plays, along with 40 pages of color and black-and-white plates. Each play is introduced by scholarly commentary from one of the volume's editors. The book also contains general background material on the Shakespearean stage and Elizabethan history.

Title: *The Complete Works of Shakespeare*
Author: David Bevington (editor)
Publisher: Addison-Wesley Publishing Company
Year: 1997
Summary: This book offers the complete, unabridged works of Shakespeare as edited by the current president of the Shakespeare Association of America. Editor David Bevington also provides an introductory essay for each play and a general introduction to Shakespeare's life, times, and stage.

Title: *Shakespeare: A Life*
Author: Park Honan
Publisher: Oxford University Press
Year: 1999
Summary: Using the little available data that exists, Honan pieces together this biographical account of Shakespeare's life.

Title: *A Shakespeare Glossary*
Author: C. T. Onions (editor)
Publisher: Oxford University Press
Year: 1986
Summary: This classic reference book defines all of the now-
obscure words used by Shakespeare throughout his plays.
The book also uses examples and gives play locations for
the words.

Title: *Shakespeare A to Z: The Essential Reference to His Plays,
His Poems, His Life and Times, and More*
Author: Charles Boyce
Publisher: Facts on File
Year: 1990
Summary: This book features over 3,000 encyclopedic
entries arranged alphabetically. It covers several areas of
Shakespeare, including history, play synopses, and critical
commentary.

Title: *The Shakespearean Stage: 1574–1642*
Author: Andrew Gurr
Publisher: Cambridge University Press
Year: 1992 (3rd ed.)
Summary: An overview of Shakespearean staging by Andrew
Gurr, one of the foremost experts in this area. The book
highlights the many different theater companies of the day
and how they performed.

Title: *Shakespeare's Book of Insults, Insights & Infinite Jests*
Author: John W. Seder (editor)
Publisher: Templegate
Year: 1984
Summary: This entertaining book covers several categories
of jabs and mockeries taken straight from the text of
Shakespeare's plays.

Title: *Everybody's Shakespeare: Reflections Chiefly on the Tragedies*
Author: Maynard Mack
Publisher: University of Nebraska Press
Year: 1994
Summary: Mack offers essays on *Romeo and Juliet, Julius Caesar, Hamlet, Othello, King Lear, Macbeth,* and *Antony and Cleopatra,* plus four chapters covering general topics. The essays are written specifically for the general reader by the author, a noted scholar.

Title: *The Meaning of Shakespeare* (2 vols.)
Author: Harold Goddard
Publisher: University of Chicago Press
Year: 1960
Summary: Originally published in 1951, this classic, hefty work of Shakespearean criticism includes essays on all of Shakespeare's plays. (Note: Because Goddard's work is in two volumes, readers who seek information on particular plays should make sure they obtain the volume containing commentary on that play.)

Videos

Title: *William Shakespeare's Romeo & Juliet*
Director: Baz Luhrmann
Year: 1996
Summary: Shakespeare's play is set in Miami against a backdrop of gang violence and MTV-style editing. Leonardo DiCaprio and Claire Danes play the lead roles in this updated version of the classic love story.

Title: *Romeo and Juliet*
Director: Franco Zeffirelli
Year: 1968
Summary: This Academy Award–winning version of the play breaks with tradition by casting two teenage actors to play the lead characters. The result is one of the silver screen's most beloved adaptations of a Shakespearean play.

Title: *Romeo and Juliet*
Director: Paul Czinner
Year: 1966
Summary: This is a ballet version filmed at the Royal Opera House. Rudolf Nureyev and Margot Fonteyn star.

Title: *Romeo and Juliet*
Director: Renato Castellani
Year: 1954
Summary: Filming took place in Italy for this lesser-known movie version of the play. This motion picture took the Grand Prix award at the 1954 Venice Film Festival.

Audiotapes

Title: *Romeo & Juliet* [Abridged]
Producer: Arkangel Complete Shakespeare
Year: 1998
Summary: This audio production features a full-cast performance by members of England's professional theater community. A rousing musical score rounds out this staging.

Title: *Romeo & Juliet*
Producer: BBC Radio Presents
Year: 1994
Summary: Kenneth Branagh and the Renaissance Theatre Company perform the play for BBC Radio. The listener is treated to the poetic sound of Shakespeare's language that would be missing from a silent reading of the text.

Title: *All the World's a Stage: An Anthology of Shakespearean Speeches Performed by the World's Leading Actors*
Producer: BBC Radio
Year: 1995
Summary: A collection of some of the finest performances of Shakespeare's famous passages. Laurence Olivier, Richard Burton, and Vanessa Redgrave are featured along with several other notable actors.

Web Sites

URL: *http://www.rdg.ac.uk/globe/research/research_index.htm*
Summary: Associated with London's Globe Theatre web site, this collection of research links offers information on the building and rebuilding of The Globe, Shakespeare's relationship to the theatre, and miscellaneous articles on theatrical traditions and practices during Shakespeare's time.

URL:
http://www.english.wayne.edu/~aune/2200W00Contents.html
Summary: This site offers introductory information for students studying Shakespeare. Offerings include tips for reading and writing about Shakespeare as well as information on individual works.

URL: *http://tech-two.mit.edu/Shakespeare*
Summary: This web site from the Massachusetts Institute of Technology features the full text of many of Shakespeare's plays in a searchable format.

URL: *http://daphne.palomar.edu/Shakespeare/*
Summary: "Mr. William Shakespeare and the Internet" offers a wide variety of links to other Shakespeare sites. "Criticism," "Educational," and "Life & Times" are just a few of the categories offered.

Software

Title: *Romeo and Juliet*
Developer: BookWorm Student Library
Grade: 7–12, Adult
Platform: Mac
Summary: The play is presented using film, sound, graphics, unabridged original texts, and relevant criticism.

Title: *Romeo and Juliet*
Developer: CenterStage
Grade: 7–12, Adult
Platform: Mac
Summary: This software presents the play as a production acted by high school–age actors. Interviews with the cast and director accompany this performance.

Title: *Romeo and Juliet*
Developer: Bride Digital Classic
Grade: 9–12, Adult
Platform: Windows and Mac
Summary: This software uses text, video, audio, and graphics to combine the original text with the performance of scenes.

Title: *Shakespeare Trivia*
Developer: Casciky Software
Grade: All
Platform: Windows
Summary: A trivia game for any ability or knowledge level. The program includes 37 plays, more than 1,200 characters, more than 400 scenes, and 500 individual quotes. Players may choose the difficulty and type of question as they test their knowledge of Shakespeare.

Title: *Shakespeare's Language*
Developer: Randal Robinson and Peter Holben Wehr
Grade: 9–12, College
Platform: Mac
Summary: This program is created to help readers identify and respond to various types of difficulty in Shakespeare's language. Problems addressed include syntactical difficulties, unfamiliar words, figurative language, unexpected and multiple meanings of words, and special connotations of words.

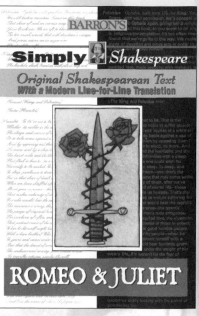